Are you looking for satisfac
away still longing for more?
just don't get it?

Read this book, it will help you.

"At Last! A genuinely useful and practical book for families and individuals who are struggling with church on Sunday morning. Tim's council is vital. He has dispensed a great deal of helpful information. The book gives hope in many ways."

— PAT DAY
1992 Kentucky Derby Winner, and Hall of Fame Jockey

"We as human beings often make life very complicated. This book will make those complications more manageable, not only for ex-Catholics, but for anyone questioning their faith. It is a good self-examination exercise."

— NORMA LAUFER
Former Catholic and Retired School Teacher

"You want answers? This book answers the core questions about life, faith and church. A must read for those who grew up in the Catholic church."

— BOB CHERRY
Senior Minister, Northeast Christian Church

"Tim Lott describes his experience of being Scripture- fed and Spirit-led from personal heartbreak and the rituals of Romanism to repentance; from denominational loyalty to a personal trust with the living Jesus for forgiveness and salvation. The by-product was reconciliation, peace and eventually, ministry. This is a moving testimony and an important book."

— J. ERNEST FREQUES
Former Priest and Author of *Reconciliation: Essays and Applications*

"A survival kit for the casual churchgoer. It brings to the forefront problems we battle with as parishioners and how to overcome them. It is convincing and practical. I wish I'd had the book twenty years ago."

— TODD OETKEN
Financial Planner, 46 Year Old Catholic

GROWING UP CATHOLIC

Tim Lott

www.GrowingUpCatholic.net

Growing up Catholic The Pursuit Of Truth, From Tradition to Satisfaction

Abundant Publishing Company
Post Office Box 770816
Coral Springs, FL 33077 U.S.A.
Orders@ www.GrowingUpCatholic.net

ISBN 978-0-9791188-3-8

Second Printing: June 2010

ATTENTION CHURCHES: Quantity discounts are available on bulk purchases of this book for educational, gift purposes, or for small groups. For information please contact Abundant Publishing Company at P.O. Box 770816, Coral Springs, FL 33077 or visit GrowingUpCatholic.net.

Publisher's Cataloging-in-Publication

(Provided by Quality Books, Inc.)

Lott, Tim, 1958-
  Growing up Catholic : the pursuit for truth : from
tradition to satisfaction : a book / by Tim Lott.
    p. cm.
  ISBN-13: 978-09-791188-3-8
  ISBN-10: 0-9791188-3-2

  1. Lott, Tim, 1958- 2. Ex-church members–Catholic
Church–Biography. 3. Protestants–Clergy–Biography.
4. Christian biography. I. Title.

BX4705.L688 2007   282'.092
                          QBI07-600076
                          Printed in USA

GROWING UP CATHOLIC

The Pursuit of Truth

from tradition to satisfaction

Tim Lott

2010

Contents

Acknowledgements

A note of special thanks and appreciation to the Adult Ministry team, which I was a part of for five years, and to all of the hard-working volunteers I served alongside at Northeast Christian Church.

A particular word of thanks and appreciation to my good friend Bob Cherry, for opening his office door in October of 1998 and leading me to Christ. My two buddies, Vicki Cherry and Shawna Donahue, for sharing life, laughs, and lunches together. And my accountability partner, Mike Gabbard, for his prayers, guidance and friendship.

I want to give thanks to Scott Eynon and the Community Christian Church staff and church family in Fort Lauderdale, Florida, for their support and prayers, particularly to Kent Mezger, Brian Beckner and Nate Bush for their encouragement.

To my wife Genora, who insisted that I write this book, thank you for your love, your patience, your courage and your belief in me when I lacked confidence in myself.

And finally, to my immediate family, thank you Dad and Mom for being open and understanding along with my younger three brothers John, Andy and Michael and sister-in-law Dottie. The journey continues!

Introduction

The French philosopher and mathematician Blaise Pascal said, "In between heaven and hell is life;" however, I would like to add to his statement and say, "In between heaven and hell is a life that is searching for a better life." Isn't that what we are all ultimately striving for—a better life than the one we have? Well, I have found it.

I grew up in Louisville, Kentucky, in a Catholic family who accepted all the Catholic traditions and beliefs. My brothers and I attended Catholic schools and one of my brothers served as a priest for eight years. It seemed that all the pieces were in place to have that "better life" but at the age of thirty-eight, I unexpectedly found myself alone without much hope. A void had existed in my life for an exceptionally long time, but I did not understand what was causing the emptiness.

At some point, we all question the path we are traveling, questioning what we were taught, or what we thought we believed. When disaster hit, I had to take a hard look at my life. Fortunately, I discovered what was missing, but the path to that remarkable discovery was a complicated one, filled with questions about my future, my faith and my identity.

In this book, I want to address some questions I had from growing up Catholic, most former and current Catholics will relate to them. This book will provide an in-depth look at some of the major Catholic traditions and beliefs, from baptism to Mary and the saints, to purgatory and the Church's doctrine.

What I have experienced has been nothing short of staggering. You, too, will benefit by discovering that same tremendous joy and peace I have found, a life of inner happiness and harmony, no matter what your circumstances may be, from feeling as if you are in a meaningless cycle filled with an emptiness within, to a rejuvenated and renewed life. My personal prayer is that God will move you through each chapter, as He has moved me these past nine years, so you can capture what I have learned in the hope of helping yourself, your family, and your friends move forward on their own adventure to finding a better way to live.

My purpose is to present clear and accurate truths regarding our beliefs as Catholics and to delve into the unpopular questions, concerns, and circumstances that we as a community of parishioners are facing today in our own lives and in the church. You will be able to use this book as a tool and a guide to explore, evaluate, and discover Jesus in your own life.

Searching For Answers

In my mind, I was confident that I knew who Jesus was, and I never doubted in my heart for a moment that I had a relationship with Him. I came to the startling realization, however, that I was missing something. As a Catholic, I could not possibly accept thinking that I did not have the authentic relationship with Christ that I sincerely believed I had. When we are asked about developing a relationship with Jesus, the immediate response is often, "Of course, I have a relationship. I attend mass, I pray, I tithe. How dare you say such a thing?" Or, "Who are you to judge if I have a relationship anyway?"

I am not a person who should be judging anyone, but my comment is made with great concern, and it comes from having been a Catholic for thirty-eight years. I understand the practices and beliefs of American Catholics. From my personal encounters and lessons in life, I have experienced truth the hard way. I did not have a true and meaningful relationship with Christ at all. But I assumed that I did, as many allege they do today.

From the awkwardness of attending a Protestant church for the first time and dealing with my proud Catholic heritage, to finding myself separated and on the verge of a divorce, my life was taking an unthinkable turn.

During that time I discovered that something was missing in my life, and it showed up as a void deep within me. I was no stranger to that void - it had been with me for years—but I passed it off as a result of pressure from the strain of everyday life.

The struggles I faced literally brought me to my knees. As it turns out, the foundation I placed my faith in as a Catholic did not prove to be infallible.

WOW! This is Different

I met my wife Genora in 1989 at a local softball batting cage, of all places. While we were dating and playing on the same co-ed softball team, she introduced me to a small church in Louisville called Northeast Christian Church. I never will forget the first time I went to a service with her one extremely warm Sunday morning in June. I turned into the parking lot and discovered the size of the building would make it impossible for me to hide in the back. At that time, the modest church had approximately seventy people in attendance at the 9:00 a.m. service. I went to church that particular Sunday with Genora only because she asked me to go. Attending another church was not something I hungrily anticipated doing. Never having attended a protestant church service before, I had no idea what to expect.

That Sunday morning, as we walked up to the church entrance, I held Genora's hand in a death grip. Leaning over, I whispered to her, "Don't leave me alone." Here I was a thirty-one-year old man clinging to her for reassurance. I was so close to her that we had difficulty walking, which brought attention to both of us. That was the last thing I wanted. One of my reservations about going to her church was that everyone would know I was different. I had the distinct impression that people were looking directly at me, as if I were wearing a large red sticker on my forehead for all to see saying, "I am new, and I am a Catholic." My perception was that everyone there would be looking at us, so leaving was not an option. I'd promised Genora I would go to church, so no need to embarrass her or myself by leaving now. Besides, we'd been spotted by the couple at the door.

As we entered the building, the couple opened the door for us and reached out to shake our hands, saying good morning and hello with big smiles on their faces. This was different from what I was use to. Nobody at my church stood at the door and welcomed me. That warm greeting helped reduce my anxiety as we walked inside. I rapidly started scanning the area around me as if I had radar, trying to feel comfortable, but being somewhat paranoid, I wanted to quickly find a seat toward the back of the small chapel. On cue, I picked up the church bulletin, not wanting to make eye contact with anyone.

I anxiously waited, hoping that the service would start soon. Then, looking around the auditorium, I noticed no statues anywhere. *That was odd,* I thought. No cross of Jesus hung over what was referred to as the stage—what I would call the altar. Instead, there was a plain, brownish two-toned wooden cross which stood over seven feet tall. I could not find a replica of Christ nailed to the cross, which I thought was strange.

Genora leaned over to me and pointed out the senior minister as he was making his way around, saying hello to everyone and shaking hands before the service. I secretly hoped he would not come our way because I did not want to be noticed. I was having enough difficulty just getting used to the surroundings. Everyone around us, however, began saying hello to Genora who politely introduced me to each of those people. To my surprise, the atmosphere inside the auditorium was jovial, unlike the somber mood I was accustomed to.

No one made the sign of the cross, no holy water to dip our hand in, no pews, no genuflecting before we sat in our chairs, no organ music, and no stained glass windows. This was dramatically different. The surroundings and layout inside were unlike what I was used to seeing in a church; it looked strangely plain.

More and more people arrived, some laughing out loud, with coffee in one hand and a doughnut or two in the other. I started to loosen up and relax a little more. As I scanned over the program, I could not keep from noticing the word drama. I leaned over to Genora to ask what drama meant on the program.

She whispered, "I will explain in a minute." At the same time, many people were gathering up front.

"Who are all of those people gathered around each other?"

"They are the worship team" she said.

"Worship team?" I gave her a puzzled look.

At that moment, those same people moved onto the stage and started to play boisterous music, immediately grabbing everyone's attention. The booming start to the service had caught me by surprise. As I jerked from being startled, the program fell from my lap. I never heard this type of "church music" before. Wow! "This is extremely unusual" I thought.

As the music played, everyone stood up and began to sing, with the words of the song flashing on an enormous white screen above the stage. I looked around and observed everyone there was singing. The music was upbeat, and the singers had wonderful voices. I thought they were a professional group paid to perform that particular Sunday morning only. I became aware that I was enjoying myself, really appreciating this new experience of church, as I tapped my hand to the beat. The music was like having a CD player in church.

After we sang for approximately fifteen minutes, the lights dimmed. The singers and band left the stage as a new group of people moved onto the stage. Not knowing what was coming next, I whispered to Genora, "What's going on now?"

"They're getting ready for the drama."

Drama! A drama in church? "You've got to be kidding!"

"Calm down and watch. Sometimes they perform a drama to go with the message."

As the lights came back up, I nervously moved around in my seat. I had never seen a drama in church. I actually became uncomfortable and edgy about the whole situation playing out before me. I was unaccustomed to that type of church service. *What in the world was I thinking in agreeing to go to church this morning?*

I was definitely out of place and on top of that, the church lacked kneelers and there were no certain times to stand, sit, or kneel. I was uncomfortable with the environment as I anxiously tried to watch the actors perform, all the while my knee moving up and down from a nervous tic. Genora finally leaned over and placed her hand on my knee to prevent it from bouncing. With all of my fidgeting, she knew I was struggling throughout the whole performance.

Finally, the drama ended and the senior minister walked up to speak. I was silently hoping it would signal a change of pace. Walking to the podium he welcomed everyone and said a brief prayer. Afterward, calmly, but with urgency in his voice, he began speaking about everyday, real-life situations. Getting my attention quickly, his message intrigued me. For the first time in the service, I could relate. He used different verses from the Bible that were projected up onto the huge screen to support what he was teaching, elaborating on the reasons why those particular verses can play a large part in one's life.

Eventually it was time for communion. As the communion tray came around to me, with no hesitancy at all, I passed it on to the person next to me. I am a Catholic, I told myself. I was taught not to participate in communion if no priest was present. Everyone else was praying during this time as soft music played throughout the auditorium.

A short time later, the senior minister came back on stage with the worship band. Ending the service, he prayed and dismissed everyone from his position at the wooden podium, but before he left, we all stood up and sang a song. You could not help but notice the words to the song; they grabbed you by the heart and placed a smile on your face. *What an excellent ending to the service*, I thought.

As we drove home afterward, I had a few questions that I wanted to get cleared up about the church service I had just experienced. I asked Genora, "Why all the pomp and circumstance for the singing? Was the band paid to play this particular Sunday or do they perform every Sunday?"

She explained, "God wants our best. Those people are volunteers who play on the worship team."

"No way are they volunteers." I said.

"They give their best when they perform for God. When we worship Him—sing to Him—we are to give our best. Sometimes it may appear like a professional production, but that is what is required to deliver excellence, so everyone can have a joyful worship experience each time they come to service."

"Well, I enjoyed the service, but the drama episode was unlike anything I have ever experienced in church before."

"I know, you were fidgety through the whole thing."

As I drove, I continued to share my thoughts with her about my first Protestant church experience. "The preaching was uncommon for what I expected at a normal church service. Honestly, the service was not what I anticipated at all. To my surprise, I connected with what the senior minister said about everyday life and the struggles we often face." Turning toward her I asked, "Did you tip him off that I was coming to church this morning?"

"No!"

"Well, it was as if he was talking directly to me." I'd turned red in the face from sinking down in my seat, being slightly embarrassed, hoping no one noticed.

"A lot of people feel that way, including me sometimes, because whatever we're dealing with in life coincides with his message. But the message is not meant to embarrass you or anybody else; it's meant to teach you," she explained.

"This is why you see all of the Bible quotes on the screen as he talks through his message. Did you notice people taking notes, including me?"

"Yes, I noticed. I thought it was a bit abnormal, so I kept silent."

"I write notes on the outline in the program so I can go back occasionally before going to bed, and look over what was taught. Doing this exercise weekly enables me to keep focused throughout the week, along with helping me grow," she said.

I laughed, "Grow? In what way?"

"Getting through those tough and stressful times in my life is not easy. Reading over what's taught in church helps me in becoming a better person and growing closer to Christ," she explained.

"So is this what they teach at your church?"

"Yes."

This was new to me, but it made sense. Genora and I continued with our conversation over lunch with me doing most of the talking and asking more questions. After dropping her off at her house, I wondered how I got to the point of enjoying a protestant church service. Desiring to explore a different church seemed illogical to me, not to mention it being another faith; this was not something a Catholic would question. I was not pushing my Catholic heritage aside; however, I was concerned about my family and friends.

What would they think of my attending a protestant church? Even so, I admitted to myself that what Genora said made me think and I found myself enjoying that church experience with the teaching and upbeat music—except for the drama. That was a bit extravagant for me.

I could not get the feeling of being uncomfortable about my

background as a Catholic out of my mind. I had issues with my faith. Although attending mass every Sunday was rare for me, I was troubled because I assumed I was somehow wrong by visiting another church. Feeling disconnected when I did go to mass was one of the immense struggles I faced when asking questions and seeking answers to the direction I was headed. *I am a devout Catholic, who has a long line of Catholics in my family*, I thought. Speculating, I wondered if my ancestors had ever questioned their own concerns of being detached at any time in their own lives. Did they feel the same void or emptiness down deep, as I sometimes felt, or did they simply ignore what bothered them by suppressing their feelings? I wondered if they'd ever wanted to seek what was missing in their lives?

On the other hand, maybe my relatives did ask questions regarding the rituals and manmade rules we followed as Catholics. If that happened, it would have been extremely difficult in the culture in which they grew up. Even in our current world, where we challenge and question everything, it's problematical. We were taught since childhood that the Catholic Church is supreme in all substance of faith and morals. Who were we, especially me, to question the priests, the bishops or even the Pope? From my early years in grade school I was under the impression that all Catholics, including my family, looked at the Catholic Church as the absolute and only true church. After all, it was what we all recited at every mass: "I believe in the one holy, Catholic and Apostolic Church," so going against and questioning the beliefs my own family had placed their absolute trust and faith in disturbed me.

The Pope is the leader of the Catholic faithful for all nations. All Catholics are asked to follow his guidance. He is considered a direct successor of the apostle Peter and is called His Holiness. He occupies the office of the Holy See. The Pope has the final say in all church matters. The papal hierarchy was developed and patterned after the Roman Empire's system of governance. All of its teachings came down from one form, the Pope himself.

For instance, if you find yourself on vacation in the south of Mexico and attending mass on a Sunday morning, you are sure to notice the church is much larger, and the language spoken is Spanish. However, you would not have a problem understanding or following the mass itself, because of the steep tradition. All Catholic churches around the world have mass basically in the same way. Any changes to that tradition must come directly from the Pope.

Those rituals are extremely important and, as a juvenile, I was taught the catechism of the Catholic Church. When a person starts to look at a different concept of church, therefore, it can be traumatic and personal. I have known many Catholics who would construct thick walls of pride to protect themselves from believing they were actually questioning some of the deeply embedded beliefs they had been taught. Consequently, many parishioners are disappointed and disconnected from the Church. They are struggling with accepting the truth, as I did.

My first experience of going to a Protestant church was a positive one, so I continued to attend church with Genora regularly. I grew more comfortable with each visit, although, I still squirmed in my seat during the dramas.

I did not realize how deep within me my Catholic tradition and its sacraments were instilled. As a result, I was not ready to give up my background yet, even though I was frustrated from not relating or connecting spiritually with the Catholic Church. If you have ever had the sensation of loneliness, even when surrounded by many people, then you understand what I was experiencing when I attended mass. That particular feeling was not something I experienced everyday. Only when life generated problems would I feel down, lonely, angry, or possibly worried and stressed about my job. These were the times when I felt the emptiness inside. I became detached when I attended Sunday mass, partly because it was not relevant to my life. I don't want to sound selfish; I was confused and often discouraged by the laws and canons that we were taught to have faith in.

I was aware of and sensitive to the fact that the mass is the most important sacrament to Catholics because of what it is believed to accomplish. The catechism describes the mass as the source and the summit of Christian life, "the sum and the summary of our faith" and "the sacrament of sacraments," which is the transubstantiation, meaning that Jesus is upon the altar as the sacrificial victim to be offered up as a living sacrifice to propitiate God's wrath against sin. So the guilt and shame I had about attending another church weighed heavily on me.

The catechism clearly spells out the church's beliefs on love and marriage, children, God, creation, humanity, life, death, the afterlife, Mary, the Church, the saints and the sacraments. With this guidance from the Church and all of its teachings, how could I possibly feel so disconnected from it? Attending mass was a spiritual time, and the Church was a place to be with God, but I did not see it happening in my life. Although my youth was filled with religion along with the sacraments and ceremonial procedures, which I practiced and participated in, why did it seem that God was missing?

Wow! This is Different

SMALL GROUP OR CLASS LEADER: Introduce yourself and ask those in the class to introduce themselves. Make sure everyone in the group has a book. Ask the group to bring their Bible each week if they have one. Use the questions below as discussion questions.

Q: If you were born and raised in the Catholic Church, what keeps you connected and part of your church community today?

Q: Do you feel as if you have a lot of religion but God seems far away? Explain you answer.

Q: Take a moment and envision your ideal church. What would need to be in place for you to feel connected?

Q: There are times when we need to take some risks. Tim shared his experience of attending a protestant church service for the first time. He was not prepared for some of the differences that he encountered. How do you think you would handle your first experience in a different faith based church? If you have already been attending a different church how was your experience? What stands out the most in your mind? What made you feel this way?

Q: Did you feel guilty for not attending a Catholic service? If yes or no, describe what made you feel this way?

Q: How did your new church experience affect you? Was it a positive or negative experience and why? Explain your answer below.

Q: Tim spoke of having an empty feeling, or void in his life in regards to church. Have you ever experienced that same feeling? Describe in detail below.

Q: Tim writes, "Although my youth was filled with religion, along with the sacraments and ceremonial procedures, which I practiced and participated in, why did it appear that God was missing?" What would your answer be to this question?

GROUP DISCUSSION QUESTION:
Q: Now that you have answered the above questions, did you find that other people in the group had similar answers and experiences to your own? Why do you think this would be possible? How did it make you feel?

Disaster Strikes Home

Genora and I married in November 1989, in the same little church she had introduced me to when we met. She always wanted a small and elegant wedding and it fit perfectly in the petite chapel. But before we were married, we both never dreamed that a mixed faith marriage could potentially be difficult for us. Despite the strong concerns and warnings from her mother and a few of her friends regarding our relationship, Genora and I held tightly to the love and care we had for each other believing we could overcome any complex obstacles that could kill a marriage. We were deeply in love and nothing was going to destroy that love between us.

For me, not identifying with the Protestant church made it difficult. Consequently, I did not understand the commitment she had to her church and sometimes felt left out. Every Wednesday evening Genora volunteered in the church kitchen helping six other women prepare a dinner for fifty or sixty families. On Sunday mornings she volunteered in the children's area. There were Bible studies she attended but I felt awkward so elected not to go. The same way I did not relate to the Protestant church, Genora did not comprehend the Catholic Church with all of its traditions I grew up following and believing in. There was no switch or knob to turn off when it came to my Catholic background and beliefs.

I continued to attend Northeast with her nearly every Sunday; however, I was a "back-row Joe" type of guy as I liked to refer to myself then. When I missed church on a Sunday, it was primarily because the NFL show started before we got home. Many times, if I elected to sleep in, however, I often found myself feeling guilty after

Genora left for church. Being at fault, I challenged myself to get up, shower and meet her at church.

That little chapel grew over the next few years to a sizable congregation, which needed a much larger auditorium with seating for over a thousand people. Like most, Genora and I had our favorite place to sit, on the end of the aisle a few rows from the back in the new auditorium.

During those years of attending Northeast Christian Church, I continued battling traditions and the pride of my Catholic background, not wanting to let go. Deep inside, I was a Catholic and I was not planning on changing. I saw no need to change.

At Northeast and at most Protestant churches, we frequently witnessed a baptism during the service. Those baptisms usually took place live in a large, elongated tub toward the back of the stage but very visible to the audience. There were also times during the service that we watched a video on two large video screens of a group of people being baptized outdoors in a nearby pool or lake. The process of being baptized was described as starting a new journey in life. As I sat observing what was taking place, I remembered saying to myself, *I am happy for them, but you will never see me getting baptized like that.* The event failed to achieve the same impact for me as it did the other people in church. Everyone in the auditorium clapped, some people even stood up and cheered, some shed tears after a person was baptized.

People at church also used the term "born again" in referring to those who had been baptized, which bothered me. *What in the world were they talking about, born again?* I'd heard that term only in reference to religious fanatics.

The fact remained, when it came to baptism, my parents elected to have me baptized as an infant. Why go through the process again? I understood the reason my parents wanted my baptism as an infant and felt comfortable with their decision.

———

Nine years had passed since our marriage in that small chapel. Everything was going fine, so I thought, during those nine years as a young couple trying to move up the status ladder. I tried to make as much money as possible by stepping out and opening doors to get a better job than the one I had. By nature, I am a determined individual, and I'd sought to impress my wife, concerned with making her happy and having her respect.

A major part of what I was trying to accomplish was proving to myself that I was capable of success. Because I had been troubled about my dyslexia, school for me did not come easily, nor did many other things in life. I was convinced by my high perception of believing that I needed to be a "somebody" to get respect. Having this important person status aided in feeding my drive. Believing my dyslexia was a detriment and a deterrent, I constantly strove to improve and better myself, no matter what. All or nothing was the way I looked at it. With the drive to succeed, I found myself with tunnel vision, only focusing on obtaining my personal goal of financial success.

Along the way to achieving my goal, however, I overlooked a lot of details, including important aspects of my marriage and what it meant to share the same dream and success with my wife. My dream of success was not exactly the same dream Genora had in mind. Genora and I were on a collision course, reality caught up with both of us in one enormous impact and our long-sought-after goal of believing nothing could separate us was destroyed and came plummeting down to wreck our worlds.

After work one late October afternoon in 1998, I walked into the house, tired as usual. On the kitchen counter I found a note that read, "I have had enough and it is over. I am leaving you. I will be staying at Debbie's" was all it said.

Realistically I should have been aware of our crumbling relationship. Genora worked very hard at her career. We were both extremely busy and often exhausted from our daily routines, which left little time for us to be a true married couple. Proper communication is essential to any successful marriage; we simply had a difficult time communicating and understanding each others needs and wants. Our priorities were not the same, and this caused internal struggles. Resolving conflict had been a difficult process for us, especially when we both shied away from confrontation with each other. Finally, it came to a point where we no longer could resolve a conflict.

There were many times Genora wanted to be alone to fill up

because she is an introvert, I on the other hand was an extrovert wanting companionship.

I should not have been shocked or astounded by what I read, but deep down I did not want to believe our situation had become as bad as it really seemed. Suddenly, I realized that everything we dreamed and hoped for came crashing down on top of me, and I fell hard. Thankful we did not have children who would be affected by our separation, all I could manage was to sit in silence alone in the house, thinking. Genora was my world. All I'd wanted to do was make her proud of me. I had to prove to both of us that I was a success. Instead, I'd managed to destroy the exact thing I'd tried so hard to achieve. Sitting on that hard kitchen floor, I was filled with deep hurt and sorrow, the type of pain that eats away deep inside your inner being, throbbing, stabbing until I physically ached.

As I sat motionless, I began to think and remember every ounce of effort I'd put forth over the years in order to get life right and marriage right. I asked myself, *What am I doing wrong that I can't make it work? I repeated, Why this, and Why now?*

I continued to sit on the floor, staring at the wall in silence. Slowly I began to understand that running my life in my own way was not working. How possibly could it, if losing the one I loved was all I had to show for it? My world had fallen apart. I was frustrated and scared, no longer having control of the situation and, worst of all, I did not know where to turn next. That was a completely new experience for me. In nearly all circumstances, I had known what to do, at least for thirty-eight years I'd thought I had. But that time, the only issue I was certain of was the act of her leaving that day. This solidified my thoughts. Leaving was something she would only do if she was not coming back.

I faced every ounce of the hurt and anguish that one experiences when severed from someone he has built a life around. I became conscious of selling the house, dividing all we owned and losing some of our friends. Only a few months earlier, Genora had expressed to me that we were like two ships passing in the night; I had my schedule, she had hers, which also included how we approached God and church.

Foolishly, not recognizing how bleak our situation was, and only trying to get ahead by focusing on what I believed to be the correct priorities in life, I'd overlooked any tribulations that crept into our lives, thinking I could take care of the problems. Obviously, I was mistaken. And it became evident that my impression of believing the relationship I had with Christ was a personal one had been more of a casual affair. I assumed that I was truly in touch with Christ. But all of the religion I grew up with gave me only a false sense of self-assurance.

Remembering the words Genora had written, I finally forced my lifeless body off the floor, after what was apparently hours. It was pitch black outside, with the house completely dark and incredibly quiet. Emotionally drained, I made my way upstairs, turned on a small dim bedroom light, and collapsed on the bed. As I lay gazing at the ceiling, the tears started to flow. At one point, I wept uncontrollably. I felt total worthlessness. Secluded in the dimly lit room, I lay there searching and struggling for answers. I wanted to reconcile the differences we both had and some how achieve the relationship we both wanted but never experienced, but how?

After maybe an hour or more, I simply rolled off the bed, laboring to my knees. I leaned over on the bed and earnestly prayed to God, humbly asking Him to show me or give me an answer. I told Him that I was tired of failing, tired of doing life my way. It was obvious that I'd gotten it wrong, no matter how much exertion I'd given to get it right. I prayed, "What should I do, and where should I turn for help?"

Lying awake that night, discouraged and depressed, wondering how I would tell my family and friends about Genora and me, I thought again about selling the house and everything else that goes with a divorce. I also realized that our different faiths contributed to having created an emotional emptiness between us. Everything raced through my mind—the hurt of losing my wife and the feeling of failure was a tremendous weight on my heart.

That night as I prayed, the oddest thing happened. After I got back to the bed, a name kept coming into my mind. Why would Bob Cherry, the name of the senior minister, keep ringing in my head? His name came to my mind repeatedly, until finally I knew in my heart that I needed to talk to him first thing in the morning about my marriage. I hardly knew Mr. Cherry, but the ringing in my head wouldn't stop. I heard the name Bob Cherry again and again. Eventually I dozed off and woke the next morning with the same clothes I had on from work the day before.

I knew calling him would be a strenuous task. When Genora and I talked to Bob about getting married nine years earlier, he'd told Genora as I sat beside her, "You should not marry Tim, because he is not a Christian." The comment certainly caught me off guard and shocked me, thinking he had stepped over the line making such a suggestion. Genora's reaction was more of a person who understood but was not going to withdraw. She said, "Tim believes in God and our different faiths would be a minor obstacle." She also admitted to knowing nothing of the Catholic faith. At the time I had no idea that our different beliefs would be questioned, although later Genora related to me that she was aware that the faith issue would be brought up.

After arriving at work that morning, I nervously called the church office. The senior minister's assistant, Shawna Donahue, answered. "Hello, Northeast Christian Church."

"May I speak to the senior minister, please?"

She kindly asked, "What does this pertain to?"

"My name is Tim Lott, and it's regarding my marriage to Genora." She put me on hold for a minute. Then Bob Cherry answered and, after a brief conversation, he agreed to meet with me the next day at 4:00 p.m.

All day and night, I tried diligently to keep focused as I nervously anticipated the meeting. In the back of my mind I still remember the words he'd spoken: "Genora, you should not marry Tim."

I glanced at the clock in my car, 3:55 p.m. My hands gripped the steering wheel tightly as I sat in the church parking lot. I was in a difficult situation and I knew stepping into that building would be excruciatingly painful; nevertheless, I opened the car door and walked into the main entrance and down the hallway to his office.

I knocked on the door and walked in. His assistant, Shawna, greeted me with a smile. She led me to another room down the hall. As we entered, I noticed how small but nicely decorated the room looked. A comfortable but private setting, with a burgundy couch and two matching chairs.

"He'll be here in a moment, Tim. Just have a seat."

The pain and embarrassment of going to the person who married us and explaining to him that we were now getting a divorce was overpowering. I could not force out of my mind those words he'd said to Genora that day and now I had to admit he was right. The hurt and disappointment of accepting that we were getting divorced was devastating but I tried to hide how I felt.

I was still confused about why his name had kept ringing in my head the night before. As I sat down, my attention was drawn to the large painting on the wall across from me. The scene was a huge, snow-capped mountain with a waterfall cascading down the side, as a deer in the green valley below was engaged in taking a cool drink of water. Looking at the painting had a calming effect and gave me a chance to rehearse what needed to be said.

A few minutes later Reverend Bob Cherry entered the room and sat down directly across from me. "Tim, in what way could I be of assistance to you today?"

My mouth was so dry I could not swallow; however, I breathed in deeply and started to explain everything. I told him, "I am exhausted from doing life my way. I have had it. After trying to make life work for so long, this is not the result I wanted. Now it has come to the point that my marriage is over. Everything I've worked for is completely lost."

Expecting Bob to tell me "I told you so" or lecture me on the spot, he paused for a moment and said "You know there is a better way to live life, Tim. You need Christ in your life. But you need an authentic relationship with Him if you want your life to change."

Pausing for a moment, I thought, *This is new to me. I've never been taught this, nor have I heard something like this before in my Catholic experience.* Looking up I said firmly, "OK, that is what I want." No turning back now. I sincerely wanted this relationship with Christ to become real. I wanted a better way to live.

He said, "You will need to get on your knees and honestly ask God for His forgiveness. You need to sincerely ask Jesus to come into your heart, Tim. But you can not do this for Genora; you need to do it for yourself."

Not bothering to wait until I got home, I went to my knees right there in that little room. In truth, a broken man went to his knees that afternoon. On my knees, I asked God to forgive me and I asked

Jesus to come into my heart. Everything around me slowed down that instant and ceased to exist. I became extremely aware that I'd hit rock bottom and that I wanted a change. I let everything go as emotion took over. Soon I was in tears. Bob knelt down beside me, placing his hand on my shoulder and he prayed out loud, "Father, I ask that you hear Tim's plea for help as he kneels before you now." Then I proceeded to ask God for His forgiveness and pleaded for Christ to come into my heart and change my life.

That moment was very powerful and moving, I was past the embarrassment of what other people may think of me being weak or emotional; that was unimportant. Showing weakness and emotion was certainly different for me, but the pride I once carried was left on the floor of the church office that day.

Gone, too, were the feelings of total despair and the thoughts of hopelessness. Before arriving in Bob's office that afternoon, I had no clue what to expect. The negative feelings of those chilling words, *"You should not marry Tim,"* was all I thought about and I expected a reprimand. But it never came. Bob did not even bring up the subject. Instead of a reprimand, he gave me the Book of John from the New Testament and suggested I read it. He also suggested we set a time to meet a week later and if I had any questions about the book, he would answer them then.

That afternoon I gained an authentic relationship. I'd started what I call an adventure with Christ, and that adventure with Him has changed my life. I remember to this day how I reacted when I left that room, feeling as if a massive boulder had just been lifted from my chest. Closing the main church door behind me as I walked to my car, I pumped my fist up and down as if I just won an important game. The enormous burden I was carrying had been removed. The weight of the world that had been on my shoulders was no longer there. That afternoon on the office floor was an incredibly humbling experience.

I realized that something astonishing had happened to me by completely turning my life over to Christ. The feeling is complicated to describe and difficult to express in words but inside I knew everything would be OK. The confidence I felt was that I was not alone to fight the struggles ahead and it was phenomenal.

The book Bob gave me explained about John the Baptist and

Jesus' teachings. Growing up, I never picked up the Bible, much less did I read it.

The only Bible teaching was from the priest reading five minutes or so during his homily at mass. To my surprise, reading the Bible for myself and discovering the history was an eye-opening experience.

The Bible does not need to be read by starting on the first page like a regular book. I started with the book of John in the New Testament. I recommend the same for anyone who is starting to read the Bible for the first time. I personally use the New International Version (NIV) study Bible.

During our second meeting, Bob told me he would be willing to meet on a weekly basis and, if I was interested go over the New Testament. Intrigued by what I'd already learned, I willingly accepted his offer. Besides, only one hour each Wednesday would be no problem and this would give me something to look forward to.

Deliberately, I worked long hours so I could keep my mind occupied, away from thoughts of the pending divorce. I did not have communication with Genora during this time, only assuming she may have known of my studies with Bob.

Being stubborn and partly embarrassed to ask help from my family or friends, I'd arrive home as late as 9:00 p.m. after working overtime with only enough time to shower and pop a meal in the microwave before going to bed. I read the workbook on the New Testament each night before setting the alarm. To my amazement, this lifted my spirits and gave me insight on how I could handle my current situation. I gained a great deal of understanding from what Jesus had asked of us through the Bible, rather than what I received from the priest when he read the Bible at mass. Quite often the reading had not coincided with anything the priest talked about at the homily. Or, the verse was read in such a small portion it made little sense.

The detailed explanations of who wrote each book in the Bible, the date it was written and where, including a brief history of the author and the role he played in Jesus' life, was particularly interesting to me. Above all, I found it noteworthy that the people who associated with and followed Jesus—the apostles Matthew, Mark, Luke, John, and Peter, were all extremely close friends of his—each wrote about what they saw first hand as soon as fifty years after Jesus' death.[1]

As simple as it may sound, that struck a vital cord with me. My grandparents, whom I miss and love dearly, have been dead for twenty-four years as I write this book. But to this day, I can unmistakably tell you about the trips we took together—fishing with my grandfather, and the many weekends I spent at their house. I remember it all as if it were the day after it happened. In a simple and yet practical way, therefore, I understood that remembering what Jesus said had to come incredibly easy for Jesus' closest friends when they wrote about and explained what He did and said.

That was the beginning of how I personally connected to the Bible, I took what Jesus' closest companions said to be true. I was reading about Jesus from those who actually heard His words, saw His miracles and walked with Him daily. They were eyewitnesses to His many teachings and the events that took His life. As a result, I began to pay strict attention when I read what Jesus taught us through the writings of the disciples and others such as Paul. The teachings of Jesus came alive for me in the Bible and meant so much more than what I had ever heard at Sunday mass, especially when John (3:3) says, "Jesus declared, I tell you the truth, no one can see the kingdom of God unless he is born again."[2]

Born again, that was the phrase I did not understand and made fun of before, believing only religious extremists or religious activists used that term. And here I read where Jesus Himself used it for us to follow as an act of renewal. I was curious wanting to investigate more of what Jesus meant by dying to your old self and being "born again." As I read that phrase, my Catholic beliefs, including my own baptism, began to come into question. No doubt, there were hard, probing questions ahead of me that I needed to address, along with many intriguing issues necessary to learn the truth about.

CHAPTER TWO

Disaster Strikes Home

SMALL GROUP OR CLASS LEADER: Review chapter one. Use the questions below as discussion questions. Encourage each person to answer these questions honestly. Ensure that the group is in a comfortable environment so they may share their answers openly.

Q: "We humans want life our own way and on our own terms. It seems as if we are not concerned about the future or anyone else. We work our own plan, our way, on our own time." Why do you believe that we desire this power to control our way of living?

Q: List a few of the ways that you control your life?

Q: Can you think of a time when you wished you had listened to someone else's advice besides your own? Explain.

Q: Have you ever been so distraught that you felt like you have hit "rock bottom" or experienced a serious setback in your life? Did you turn to someone for help or try to work it out on your own? What was the outcome?

Q: When you were distressed, did you pray? Why, or why not? To whom did you pray?

Q: When you were troubled, did you find yourself searching for monetary things to help you feel better, such as, shopping for new clothes, planning a trip or buying a new car? Give an example.

Q: If you were to rely on Jesus instead of yourself, what do you think the result would be?

LEADER: Facilitate a discussion on the following quote.

> "God trusts us to reach out to Him. If not, He will let us go to our own natural selves, which is disastrous."
> -Dr. Harry W. Schaumburg

Can we trust ourselves to reach out to Him in bad times?

Do you reach out in good times as well?

What does this quote say about our own hearts?

Identifying The Evidence

When I was in the first grade, the mass was spoken in Latin. At six years old, I could not understand a word of Latin. In 1962, the Vatican II changed the language of the mass from Latin to English. The communities of parishioners were elated about the new format, including me; however, some people disagreed and wanted to preserve the old Latin tradition of the mass. In a gesture to be congenial to the congregation, another modification was made: the altar itself was turned around and moved toward the people. Now the priest looked out onto the congregation instead of having his back to them, which was a necessary and prudent change. Two dramatically important modifications took place for Catholic church-goers in America that year. I cannot possibly imagine what Catholic churches would be like today if those changes had not been made.

Those transformations were straightforward and simple. To understand the reasoning behind the adjustment in policy, however, there are issues and questions about the Catholic Church that continue to be in doubt. This is causing parishioners to question their own faith and re-examine the loyalty they give to the church.

Changes ultimately do take place over time in order to keep up with the changes or needs of the people and culture but change breeds controversy. Whenever traditions and beliefs are questioned, some people will likely be upset or offended. I, myself began to have questions and doubts, not because of a lack of love for the church, but because I felt disconnected. Over the next few chapters our journey takes us on a fact-finding adventure seeking out answers to those hard-to-ask questions. I was at a point in my life when I needed to search and confront the truth by examining the facts for myself.

Facing The Facts

Suppose your doctor discovered you had cancer, or a family member told you he or she was terminally ill? How would you react in that situation? What would you say? How would you feel? In times like those, we actually wish we could be super-human. Like it or not, eventually, there will come a point in all of our lives when we will have to face difficult circumstances. You may be facing them now. Are you prepared, and are you equipped to handle those situations?

When I started my fact-finding, I asked hard questions about my faith and myself. A Catholic did not consider leaving the Church to attend a Protestant church because they disagreed with certain beliefs or practices. But people are leaving the Catholic Church and for an assortment of reasons.

The most common are outdated principles, doctrinal issues, mistrust, questioning the infallibility of the Pope, sexual misconduct among the church leaders and the church's refusal to recognize second marriages. In fact, Catholic marriages have fallen by one-third since 1965. The annual number of annulments has soared from 338 in 1968 to 50,000 in 2002.[1]

A strong debate exists as to whether women should be allowed to be priests. In 1965, 1,575 new priests were ordained in the United States. But in 2002, this number plummeted to 450. In 1965, only one percent of the U.S. parishes were without a priest, while in 2002 this number was fifteen percent. On April 4, 2005, CNN reported that "Thousands Pay Respect to Pope; Catholics Welcome Change in Practices." A CNN/USA Today/Gallup poll described what American Catholics were thinking when looking to the future and looking at a new Pope. Fifty-five percent of Catholics said that the next Pope should allow women to be priests. And 63 percent of American Catholics surveyed said the church's policy on male-only priests should be reversed.[2] In the same broadcast, CNN reported that 78 percent of Catholics polled said the next Pope should allow birth control. In addition, 49 percent believed the church should change its teachings on divorce.[3]

The division within the Catholic Church in this country is real. A 2001 American Religious Identification Survey (ARIS) found that 17 percent of baptized Catholics leave the church, compared with an average of 16 percent for Americans of all faiths.[5]

In a publication by Fr. Joseph A. Sibra released in 2008 shows 23.9% of the US adult population (or 53,775,000) identifies itself as Catholic. The survey notes that this percentage is roughly the same as it was in 1972. On face value, this does not look too bad compared with Protestant losses as noted. In fact, massive Catholic losses have been hidden by the large number of Catholic immigrants. Of the present 23.9% of adults who call themselves Catholic, about 23% of that number (or 12,368,250) are immigrants, mostly Hispanic. Massive losses of native-born Catholics have not only been significant but in fact staggering, so much so, that those who conducted the survey wrote in their analysis, 'Catholicism has lost more people to other religions or to no religion at all than any other single religious group.'

10.1% of the adult population in the United States now consists of people who have left the Catholic Church for another religion or for no religion. To put it another way, one out of every 10 people in the United States (or 22,725,000) is an ex-Catholic.

The misconduct of priests has only intensified the frustration. The USA Today/AP survey of U.S. Catholic dioceses conducted by the Associated Press, dated February 10, 2004, found that 1,341 clergy members have been accused of molesting children since the 1950's.[4] On April 7, 2010, reports by CNN News (denied by the Vatican) suggested Cardinal Joseph Ratzinger– now Pope Benedict XVI - tried to contain the scandal within church walls. In all fairness, however, one needs to be conscious that the problem with the clergy is not confined to the Catholic Church.

I knew people were leaving the church, and I knew about the confrontational judgments regarding church policies and practices.

But they were in addition to my reasons of feeling such disapproval toward the Catholic Church, but that was because I was lacking spiritual growth from the mass, something that became increasingly apparent to me as I dealt with my pending divorce. Even though I now attended a Protestant church, I still considered myself a Catholic. Now, I was contemplating walking away from my Catholic faith altogether and this brought on a whole new complexity of concerns.

The devotion to certain mystic beliefs and papal leadership is something all Catholics have grown up with and accepted without question. I fell into the same category and was at a critical crossroad. For the longest time, I thought I was the only person whose life had a void when it came to church, religion or God. It was taboo to express outwardly that something was missing when it involved how we related to the mass. That was nothing more than self-centered thinking on my part. As you have read by the statistics, I was not alone in the search for filling that void.

We are not battling our frustrations, disappointments or bewildered heart single-handedly either, but, until our zeal for discovering truth is stronger than any other passion, we will continue to arrange life according to our own choices and not God's.

I began to retrace in my mind the repetitious act of attending Sunday morning mass—going through the motions—and wondering if there was more to what I had been exposed to all my life as a parishioner. You start to wonder and ask yourself, why am I going to church at all? Church on Sunday mornings was not fulfilling; instead, this became a routine. I found myself despondent, uninspired by following the church's man-made guidelines, traditions, and rituals.

I came to an insightful understanding while reflecting on my faith: most Catholics have a Catholic heritage but little else. Many will disagree, some will be unconvinced, and yet others will be angered by that statement. Being a former Catholic, I stood back and realistically examined our Catholic heritage in close detail, discovering we had only enough religion to believe that we did not need a personal relationship with Jesus. This may sound critical; however, by probing our traditions and manmade rites, we get the false impression of deep spirituality. Subsequently, when a tragedy or crisis strikes, or we find ourselves battling circumstances beyond our control, the emptiness that once had been buried deep within us now comes oozing to the surface. Confused on how to stop the flow of worthlessness from overtaking us, we search for something that our faith cannot provide, often replacing that void with temporary pleasures. In the beginning of my own search, I kept my blinders on letting my background interrupt me from seriously making choices about moving forward spiritually, and the possibility of being baptized by immersion in a Protestant church. In fact, I did not consider it.

Nothing was wrong with my Catholic baptism when I was an infant, or the traditions I was brought up practicing. My parochial schooling enabled me to pray in school and develop completely as a Catholic being taught the catechism of the church. My parents were good, honest people who grew up trusting their faith and its rituals.

The friends I grew up with were Catholic, all good, decent people with common beliefs and devotion to the church.

So what was particularly wrong with my background, nothing, nothing at all. Nonetheless, the amount of religion I received failed to help me move closer to God. In other words, I identified with the sacraments and participated in them. I trusted the ceremonial rituals and customs by following the church's teachings. I prayed and tried to be a good all-around individual. But by doing all of this, I did not have a true relationship with Christ at all. I honestly believed I did, though, and would argue heatedly with anyone who assumed otherwise.

I do believe that there are Catholics who have a sense of closeness with Christ, but I sometimes wonder how real and meaningful is their relationship? Forgive me for sounding as if I am judging anyone by that statement but understand I had relentlessly thought my companionship with Him was authentic and real as they come until my own misfortune struck.

I don't mean to repeat myself but it is important to point out from my experience, when we are lonely, angry, stressed, hurt, or feeling hopeless, we naturally turn to our belief system, however, when that structure is not sound, the majority of us turn to ourselves for answers and guidance. This can be disastrous and in the long run it is. Society has done its part in encouraging people to take charge by conquering their own lives and going for all the gusto in life. The pride in ourselves and in our belief system becomes our focal point in believing that we actually do have life under control. All the while, that void within slowly oozes out as we continue to suppress the emptiness; ignoring the obvious and believing we are strong enough ourselves to over come it. Before long, you find yourself moving in a vicious circle, not caring to discover why, but only sinking deeper into degradation, ever dependent on yourself and the customary rituals and traditions you grew up on.

Religion is not our destination, and pride should not block our salvation; our goal should be to live and love as Jesus exemplified, so we may be with God at our final destination. Some feel much safer following what the catechism teaches, rather than taking the time to examine the principles and ethics as churchgoers today. I needed to examine thoroughly the doctrine I was taught, understanding my foundational make-up completely before I was to make such a serious decision as giving up my Catholic faith. The question of why, as a Catholic, such a deep void existed within me was crucial to understand. What significantly disturbed me was knowing that many people feel that same emptiness as I had experienced, but they are unsure of what to do about it. The sad realization is most people do nothing only accepting the situation that they are in.

I did not write this book to persuade you to become a Protestant, nor did I open up a particularly private and sensitive part of my life to undermine or degrade any religion, especially the Catholic religion. I have many Catholic friends, and I dearly care about each one of them. Condemning someone's beliefs does no one any good. My only intention is to help build bridges and answer questions that may be keeping you from taking the next step in your journey of discovering a better way to live. Each of us may be moved by the spirit, no matter how loving or hateful we may be. God's love for us is one of mercy because of Jesus and what He has done for us on the cross. Our creator blessed each of us with a free will and choice. The important question is, will we turn toward Jesus or away from Jesus? Our actions on earth right now are our judgment.

Facing The Facts

SMALL GROUP OR CLASS LEADER: Review chapter two. This is the beginning of section two. Ask the group members what have they learned up to this point? What would be his or her biggest take-away from the first two chapters? Use the following questions to discuss openly.

Q: Do you agree with Tim's statement, "Many Catholics have enough religion to believe they do not need a personal relationship with Christ?" Explain your thoughts.

Q: Do you feel that the amount of religion you receive moves you closer to God? Yes or No? Why do you feel this way? Explain.

Q: If we are honest, our pride plays a big part in our belief. Has your pride led you to heated discussions or arguments when speaking about your beliefs? Now read James 4:6. "God opposes the proud but gives grace to the humble." What can you learn from this short verse?

Q: Has pride played a part in your spiritual growth as it pertains to visiting another church, holding on to traditions, or seeking a relationship with Christ? Explain why it has, or why it has not.

Q: Is pride standing in your way today?
Pride leads to arguments, bad decisions and destroys those around us. The Lord despises pride. In Jeremiah 29:13, the Lord says, "You will seek me and find me when you seek me with all your heart." Are you honestly seeking a personal adventure with Christ?

SMALL GROUP OR CLASS LEADER: Ask the group to share their thoughts on the following two statements:

Church people place God in a box called a building. They are not letting Him out of the box by their standards and rules. And we do not let Him out of the box to become part of our everyday lives.

Adults find it harder to let Him out of the box because we feel we know everything.

THINK ON THIS:
"Either we look after ourselves with a blatant, justified self-interest, or we work hard to keep everyone in our world happy with us to prevent criticism, abuse or abandonment."
-Dr.Larry Crabb

Purgatory - Temporary Punishment

*"We only have God to fear. Not a temporary hold over
filled with sorrow and pain."*

-Tim Lott

When I was a youngster, each night before going to bed, I would leave the clothes I was going to play in stacked on a chair as if I were a fireman, so when I arrived home from school I could be dressed and back out the door in less than a minute. After riding the school bus and being dropped off in the afternoon, I rushed into the house, changed clothes as fast as I could, sprinting outside to play ball with my friends. Many times, however, I was given a list of jobs around the house that needed to be completed before I went out to play. On most occasions, I moaned and groaned about doing those time-consuming, monotonous tasks. Each time I moaned, my mom would say, "Offer it up to the poor souls in purgatory."

Her words certainly did not make me feel better at the time; nevertheless, I wondered, why do those people need to visit purgatory before going to heaven anyway? How long are they stuck there? I did pray for the "poor souls in purgatory" as a child. I remember praying, "Please God give each person a drink of water to cool off. Will you remove him or her from that hot, miserable, worthless place soon?"

I can clearly see the dramatic picture I had painted in my mind of what purgatory looked like. Purgatory was not a pleasant location to reside at anytime. I assumed it was a supernatural place located somewhere in deep space, between earth and heaven. Living in such a habitual dwelling was unbearable, filled with torment and misery for millions of people. In my mind, the people in purgatory were only allowed to stand or kneel on the ground. No luxuries were there, no chairs, no ball games, no animals, nothing; people prayed for months uninterrupted before asking to be let out. In my childlike estimation, I believed it took a couple of years before God would rescue them. No one smiled and no one spoke. I pictured bright orange flames perpetually shooting out from the ground covering the entire area, much like an enormous gas barbeque grill. Hordes and hordes of people were gathered as far as the eye could see, perspiring due to the intensity of the heat and overcrowding. No water existed in purgatory, not even salt water.

I rationalized those people were not in hell; for that reason no one received real burns or died; they were merely in desperate agony. Purgatory was a temporary holding area where people were protected from the flames but not from the sweltering heat or anguish. It was well known that everyone in purgatory had committed some sort of sin, so they had to pay the price of suffering until those sins were compensated for. Until that time, no one was allowed into heaven.

Purgatory frightened me just as much as going to hell frightened me, although as an adult, I no longer believed in purgatory. It is a fictitious place. I came to be fearful of purgatory because of the Council of Trent's accepting the twelve books of the apocrypha as being true in scripture. As a result, I was taught about purgatory from a young age, as most of you were, too. Purgatory is mentioned in the book of Maccabees, which is not found in the Protestant Bible. Those additional books are not considered to be divinely inspired. When I learned this fact, I became angry and wanted to understand why I was led to believe in such a place as purgatory. I found the answer in the Decrees of the Council of Trent.

The following is the Twenty-Fifth session Decree on Purgatory, stating, "Since the Catholic Church, instructed by the Holy Ghost, had followed the sacred writings and the ancient traditions of the Fathers, taught in sacred councils and recently in this ecumenical council that there is a purgatory, the souls there detained are aided by the suffrages of the faithful and chiefly by the acceptable sacrifice of the altar. The holy council commands the bishops that they strive diligently to the end that the sound doctrine of purgatory, transmitted by the Fathers and sacred councils, be believed and maintained by the faithful of Christ, and be everywhere taught and preached."[1]

The misguidance of the doctrine in this area is detrimental to the Catholic Church by proclaiming such a place even exists. This is an example of man-made beliefs that have nothing to do with what Jesus has taught us.

After a period of time, people start to question such beliefs. For example, Bob and Josie German left the church at the age of fifty. Bob said, "My wife and I once attended a testimony meeting at the local Baptist church. We heard the impressive story of how God had changed the speaker's life." He had recently become a minister, a far cry from his previous lifestyle with the Hell's Angels motorcycle club. At the luncheon after the service, we spoke with a missionary witnessing to Catholics in Canada. He explained how he went house to house telling the people there about "God's simple message of Salvation." We had never heard that expression before. He showed us some verses from Scripture - John 3:16; 1 John 5:11, 12; Romans 5:8 - explaining about the assurance of salvation through faith in Jesus. What a drastic change from the Catholic teaching about purgatory, good works, and indulgences. In the weeks that followed, we heard many sermons based on the scripture given in this church. We had decided this is the type of spiritual food we needed for the rest of our lives.[2]

I have spoken to Catholic friends who've shared that they do not believe in purgatory. I even asked my mother what she thought about purgatory. After all, it was my mom who told me to offer my complaining up for their souls. Her reply to my question was, "Come on, Tim. I'm smarter than to be led around by the nose with that type of belief."

I laughed at her comment, hoping she didn't accept that such a place existed. Her comment, however, helped me to comprehend, to a greater extent, how people only cherry-pick what they want to follow in the Catholic Church. Most Catholics today have become buffet church-goers, tending to choose what they like, then move on. I stood in the buffet line myself for many years.

The Church's tradition on the subject of purgatory, wherein the eternal destiny of the dead are able to be influenced by the prayers of the living, has not been accepted as spiritually inspired or scriptural fact. The only popular biblical argument comes in the scripture of 2 Maccabees 12:38-46, from the apocrypha: "Turning to supplication, they prayed that the sinful dead might be fully blotted out for if he were not expecting the fallen to rise again, it would have been useless and foolish to pray for them in death." You will not find purgatory in the Bible; there is a single reference to prayer for the dead in the New Testament, which is, "May the Lord have mercy on the family of Onesiphorus when he stands before the Lord on the great day, may the Lord grant him mercy!"[3]

The Protestant faith and the Catholic faith both believe Jesus is the son of God. He was sent from God to die on the cross for our sins. He arose from the dead and sits at the right hand of God. At this point, the beliefs diverge. The Protestant church-goer believes that what Jesus said in the Bible is true. That is, He paid the full price for our sins, and we no longer have to carry that burden with us. Through God's grace alone, He has forgiven us, and we do not need to pay back penance in any manner. Furthermore, purgatory is not suggested or mentioned by Jesus or the apostles, nor is it described anywhere in the Old or New Testaments.

The Catholic Church believes that Jesus' death on the cross was not enough. More penance was needed to pay for those sins that are committed. If that penance is not paid on earth, it will be paid in purgatory. The catechism of the Catholic Church says, "That cleansing fires of purgatory exist for the punishment of their sins so as to achieve the holiness necessary to enter the joy of heaven."[4] The Church purports that you must be pure to enter into heaven; however, we all fall short of perfection with God. We all have sin, but at the Council of Trent it was declared, "If anyone says that after the reception of the grace of justification the guilt is so remitted and the debt of eternal punishment so blotted out to every repentant sinner that no debt of temporal punishment remains to be discharged either in this world or in purgatory before the gates of heaven can be opened, let him be anathema."[5] Banished from the church.

In 1967, Pope Paul VI issued an encyclical on indulgences entitled Indulgentiarum Doctrinal. Pope Paul VI stated, "The doctrine of purgatory clearly demonstrates that even when the guilt of sin has been taken away, punishment for it or the consequences of it may remain to be expiated and cleansed. In fact, in purgatory the souls of those who died in the charity of God and truly repentant, but who had not made satisfaction with adequate penance for their sins and omissions are cleansed after death with punishments designed to purge away their debt through prayer, the exchange of spiritual goods, and penitential expiation."

If this is true, then I must be telling Jesus his death was not enough and our sins were not removed by His death. Who are we to think that mere mortals have to do more than what Jesus had been sent to do by God Himself? He cleansed us of all sin. In Matthew 20:28, Jesus said, "Your attitude must be like my own, for I, the Messiah, did not come to be served, but to serve, and to give my life as a ransom for many."[7]

After discovering the truth in this area, in my mind I saw myself kicking sand in the face of Jesus. Saddened I was taught through my Catholic faith that we must perform extra penance, I searched in the Bible for additional evidence for what happens when we sin. I turned to Timothy 2:13, which reads, "If we are faithless, [God] will remain faithful, for he cannot disown himself."

What does this verse mean? It appears to give us a license to sin, but that is not the case at all. Speaking with Bob during our weekly meetings, I learned that just because I accepted Jesus as my Lord and savior and was baptized by immersion, it does not mean I will not sin again. It's foolish to think so. When I sin, God is still faithful to me. If I turn away from Him because of lack of faith or act as if I disown God by doing what I know is wrong -sinning- He will in turn disown me. Verse 12 in 2 Timothy says, "If we disown Him, He will also disown us." God does not promise to save those who are faithless- He promises to be faithful to them when they call on Him. When we turn away from God by sinning, He is still faithful to all of us. God does not go back on His word even when we are faithless through sin. He unconditionally loves us and will come to us-but only if we ask.

The apostle John said, "The blood of Jesus, His son, purifies us from all sin."[8] When I turn my back to God by sinning, I must go to God and confess my sin asking for forgiveness, making a strong effort not to sin—or turn away from Him again.

CHAPTER FOUR

Purgatory - Temporary Punishment

SMALL GROUP OR CLASS LEADER: Review chapter three. By this time in the study, members of the group or class should be getting to know one another; encourage each person to express his or her personal feelings as he or she answers the questions below. This is an important element in learning from others' experiences. Assist in locating the Bible verses from the study questions.

Q: Have you stood in the buffet line, as it pertains to the type of church-goer you are, picking and choosing what to believe or what not to believe? Explain your thoughts.

Q: Do you believe in purgatory? Why or why not?

Q: What condition affecting all humanity is described in Romans 3:23?

Q: Read Romans 6:23. What results from sin?

Q: Read John 11:25. What does Jesus promise?

Q: Do you feel that Jesus has paid the full price for our sins? What reasons can you give? Explain below.

Q: In Matthew 20:28, he said, "Just as the Son of Man did not come to be served, but to serve, and to give his life as a ransom for many." And in John 3:17, John said, "For God did not send his Son into the world to condemn the world, but to save the world through Him." What are both Matthew and John saying about Christ in these two statements?

Q: According to Romans 8:35-39, what can cut us off from Christ's love?

Q: Through God's grace alone, He has _____us.

THINK ON THIS: God is not a category. He can be trusted every day. Even so, you will be tempted and forget He is there. Do not be intimidated to ask questions as you search to figure out what direction you need to pursue. The facts are essential to examine.

Confession - Or Compensation?

"If you walk in the path of Darkness, you cannot help but to hold hands with evil."

-A death row inmate

If we were brutally honest with each other, the majority of those who are Catholic and those of us who are former Catholics would say, I am not comfortable when it comes to telling my sins to a priest in the confessional box.

During my exploration to find answers to questions of certain practices, it was vital for me to look at what the Catholic Church's guidelines are regarding confession. I probed into what the Church's canon said on the subject.

The fourteenth-session, Canons Concerning The Most Holy Sacrament of Penance states: "If anyone denies that sacramental confession was instituted by divine law or is necessary for salvation; or says that the manner of confessing secretly to a Priest alone, which the Catholic Church has observed from the beginning and still observes, is at variance with the institution and command of Christ and is a human contrivance. Let him be anathema."[1]

Here the Church is stating that if the faithful Catholics do not agree with what it has declared (confessing to a Priest alone), then they can consider themselves banished from the church. Anathema means to be banished, cut off from, or put out. If I did not tell my sins to a priest, I was anathema from the Catholic Church, a fact I was unaware of before researching facts for this book. What the canon states is a serious matter; I would have been banished from the Catholic Church long ago. I wonder how many of you are in the same predicament.

When going to confession, knowing the type of sin you are guilty of committing was important. Why? Because the type of sin determined whether I needed to go to confession right away, or if I could wait awhile. I questioned this theory about the types of sin, even when I was younger, not because of the magnitude or seriousness of the sin, but because I was terrified of the confessional box. Not until I attended a Protestant church did I find that all sins are equal. Those of us who grew up Catholic considered the two different levels of sin: venial and mortal.

The church taught three things are necessary for a sin to be mortal. They are:

1. It needs to be a serious matter.
2. Knowledge or firm belief that the act is seriously wrong prior to committing the act.
3. Full consent of the will.

All three conditions must be present simultaneously for a sin to be considered mortal; otherwise it is a venial sin. If you were unaware the act was seriously wrong, you are not guilty of having committed a mortal sin. If you did not will the act, for example, if you were forced or if it was in a dream, if you were impaired or emotionally distraught or terrified, etc., you are not guilty of the act committed. Furthermore, all mortal sins committed since your last confession must be confessed by both type and number, i.e., the kind or "name" of the sin and how many times it was committed. If there is a mortal sin from the past, and it happened to be forgotten and not confessed, once remembered it should be confessed at the next confession.

Venial sins, however, are not sins at all, so they do not need to be confessed, even though confession is encouraged. For example, you accidentally dropped your wife's beautiful glass vase on the floor and said, "Damn it to hell" in anger. The Encarta Dictionary defines a venial sin as "a sin that does not deprive the soul of divine grace, either because it was not serious or because it was committed without intent or without understanding its seriousness."

In the book *Canons and Decrees of the Council of Trent*, English translation by Rev. H.J. Schroeder, published by Tan Books 1978, we read, "Venial sins, on the other hand, by which we are not excluded from the grace of God and into which we fall into more frequently, though they be rightly and profitably and without any presumption declared in confession, as the practice of pious people evinces, may, nevertheless, be omitted without guilt and can be expiated by many other remedies."[2]

Apparently, a sin, which maybe considered an imperfection that a person committed during the day, or at anytime for that matter, are simple mistakes, not willful actions for penance. The whole explanation of types and seriousness of sin became confusing to me, including if I elected not to see a priest for confession within one year, this was considered a sin. But since I elected not to see a priest for confession, I considered this a venial sin and placed it in the imperfection category.

Wanting a clearer explanation of sin, I found the factual definition is "any act or thought that is against the way God wants us to act or think". Paul placed this in perspective, in Romans 3:20, when he said, "Therefore no one will be declared righteous in His sight by observing the law; through the law we become conscious of sin."[3] In God's eyes, a sin is a sin, no matter how large or small. In other words, the seriousness of the sin itself or the category man tries to place it in makes no difference.

After returning home one Sunday morning, not long after I started going to Northeast, I asked my wife, "What do you do about confession at a Protestant church? You don't have the confessional boxes we have."

In a simple way she explained, "We go straight to God in prayer and repent our sins to Him when they happen. He knows our hearts; He also knows if we are truly sorry with a sincere and contrite heart for what we have done or said. Consequently, we don't need to make an appointment to see someone; we go to God in our quiet time, wherever we happen to be. And that's what I try to do."

I explained to her that my experience with confessionals were not good memories. When I was growing up, I was absolutely terrified of getting ready to go into the confessional box. Most confessionals were located in the rear of the church, which made it easier to talk to the priest and not disturb other people. Usually confessionals are made of dark grain wood, and you entered through a curtain or sliding wooden door. As you walk inside the small compartment, you immediately notice a kneeler. When you kneel, a small red light appears outside on top of the entryway indicating it is occupied. The confessional is reasonably dark inside, but you are capable of seeing. When the priest is ready to hear your confession, he slides open a little wooden door that has a screen so only your voice can be heard; he does not see you and you cannot see him.

Our entire grade school would take two days and visit the confessional at Easter. I never took this lightly as a youngster. In the third grade, when it was our class's turn to go, my hands started to sweat. I knew that I had to come up with something to say when I got inside that obscure box. But what sinister sins are you able to confess to a priest when you're only in the third grade? So I made things up to cover myself as I stood in line waiting for the red light to go off.

Standing still and waiting as each person took his or her turn was nerve-wracking. I was wringing my hands and wiping the small droplets of sweat from my forehead. I'm only in third grade, and I'm feeling all of this tremendous pressure. While standing in line I thought to myself, *what if I forget what to say?*

"Ultimately, it was my turn. I hurriedly walked in, slid the curtain closed and kneeled on the padded kneeler, waiting for the screen door to open. Time seemed to crawl. Eventually the small door slid opened and I said, 'Forgive me, Father, for I have sinned.' I remember to this day how scared I was. My mouth was so dry I could barely move it to talk."

"What did you say to him?"

I would say "I fought with my three brothers, but it was not my fault." Explaining and trying to clarify that, I did not start the fight. Putting it in plain words, being the oldest of four boys all three of my brothers would team up against me."

"You told him that" she asked?

"Yes. He would ask, 'Is that all'? I would simply say 'Yes,' and Father would give me 10 Hail Mary's and four Our Fathers to say as my penance. In addition, before I left the booth, he would say, 'Don't fight with your brothers." I explained to Genora that eventually, even as a boy, I went to God for forgiveness and discontinued going to the priest. Not because I thought he did not listen to my appeal, but I never got over the fear of the confessional, even as an adult.

Looking back, I could have been called a hypocrite for calling myself a Catholic when I decided not follow all of the laws of the Church. The book Fast Facts on Roman Catholicism, by John

Ankerberg and John Weldon, published by Harvest House in 2004, explains penance this way: "The sacrament of penance is designed specifically to deal with sins committed after baptism. Why, because the grace that is received or infused in baptism can be entirely lost by mortal—"deadly"—sin. Mortal sin is held to be deadly because it literally destroys the grace of God within a person, making salvation necessary again."[4]

Here is a practical way to look at paying penance. God, the judge of all the earth, brings each of us forward and pronounces that we all are guilty of sin. The general charge is stated, "The world is found guilty." We are given an opportunity for a hearing, however. The problem is that everyone is guilty, so who is capable of representing us? No one is. The verdict given is final—guilty as charged. The judge has spoken and has condemned the world with no chance of appeal. God's wrath will be revealed; hence, we need a world savior. God is truly a God of love, so He appoints one to represent us. Now He asks, "Is there anyone to represent these sinners?" The Son of God says, "Yes, I am here to represent them. True, they committed sins and they are guilty as charged, but I bore their guilt on the cross. I died in their place so they might go free. I am their righteousness." Consequently, the judge sets them free.

Jesus died in our place, and we all fall short of being pure, as far as God is concerned. The truth is, we sin because it is our nature, and the proper punishment must be given to us; however, God loves us so much that He sent Jesus to endure the punishment. That is precisely what He did on the cross, paying our reprimand in order for us to go free. Contrary to Catholic belief, we do not need the granting of indulgences as I was (we) were taught.

I think many Catholics find it difficult to relate to what the Church has taught with regard to the sacrament of penance. If parishioners as a whole do not have a problem with going to confession, they must ask themselves a direct and honest question. What is their excuse for not going to the priest and receiving penance? The Church hierarchy and canon laws tell us it is vitally important to confess our sins to a priest. The sacrament of penance offers a new possibility to convert and to recover the grace of justification.

So I wondered what has stopped so many from going to a priest and confessing their sins? Could it be the lack of time in our busy world? Were the parishioners not taking full responsibility for what the church's doctrine teaches? Maybe embarrassment had become a major issue. On the other hand, possibly the confusion over mortal and venial sin kept people at bay.

One of the significant lessons I have discovered is that we all need to look deeply within ourselves and ask, if you are not following the Catholic doctrine or participating as you are expected to and in the way indicated by your faith, then, realistically, you are merely going through the motions and calling yourself a Catholic. Think about this, are you only practicing and choosing what is important to you when it comes to confession? If that is true, could you be called a hypocrite? I personally struggled with this question for the longest time and realized I could have easily been called a fraud or hypocrite. I did not follow many of my own foundational beliefs, which made me a Catholic, yet I still called myself a Catholic.

Not until I was studying with Bob Cherry, who had become a good friend, did I learn that praying directly to God and confessing my sins to Him was OK. I had learned from the Church's catechism that if I decided not to perform the sacrament of penance, I had committed a mortal sin and was immediately headed to eternal punishment in hell.

I found none of that to be true. Christ paid for our sins: no matter how small, how grave or how mortal those sins were. In Ephesians 1:7, the apostle Paul says, "In Him we have redemption through His blood, the forgiveness of sins, in accordance with the riches of God's grace." In addition, Paul again explains in Colossians 2:13, "When you were dead in your sins and in the un-circumcision of your sinful nature, God made you alive with Christ. He forgave us all our sins."[5] What breathtaking news that was to a person who grew up Catholic, concerned about rarely ever going into the confessional and confessing to a priest.

"No one can be justified apart from the sacrament of penance"— the confession of sin to a Roman Catholic priest, receiving his absolution and performing the required penance,[6] is what our catechism teaches us.

In other words, Christ's death on the cross was not enough, and we must do more penance than Christ's payment on the cross. Learning this made me feel a bit uneasy. Doing more penance in order to wipe away my sins so I would regain Gods grace troubled me a great deal; however, by reading Titus 3:5 in the New Testament, I had more confirmation that His death was enough. Paul says, "He saved us, not because of righteous things we had done, but because of his mercy. He saved us through the washing of rebirth and renewal by the Holy Spirit."[7]

In summary, what I have learned about confessing is that we can approach God directly. When we approach Him with our sins, He wants a person with a sorrowful heart in front of Him on his or her knees, not a sacrifice from doing penance or saying a certain number of Hail Mary's or Our Fathers repeatedly. That does not convey what the heart should actually be feeling or expressing to God. Our chants of different prayers as penance are nothing but lost words.

Knowing that Jesus removes the guilt of sin, the penalty of sin and the power of sin along with the sinner's actual liability to eternal wrath because of sin, made me take a more exhaustive look at what I was taught to believe. For some strange reason, though, I had a sense of guilt, as if I needed a pardon for questioning my beliefs. I discovered an article in *"What the Bible is all About,"* by Dr. Henrietta C. Mears, published by Regal Books 1997, which helped me get over my guilty feelings. She writes, "When God looks at us, He sees no righteousness. When He looks at us in Christ, He not only sees improvement, but also perfection, for God sees only His own righteousness, Jesus Christ."[8]

Confession - Or Compensation?

SMALL GROUP OR CLASS LEADER: Review chapter four.
As members enter the room, ask them to write down what they need to confess to God in the space provided below. They do not have to share what they write. Before the end of this session, give a few minutes of quiet time for everyone to go to God with the sins they have written down in the last question.

Q: Which of the above do you feel are mortal sins or venial sins?

Q: The definition of sin is any act or thought that is against the way God wants us to act or think. Before reading this chapter, were you aware that all sins are equal in Gods eyes? Explain why or why not below.

Q: Think about the last time you went to confession. How did it make you feel before and after you went into the confessional? Explain your feelings at that time, even if it was more than a few years ago.

Q: After leaving the confessional and saying your penance, did you have a sense that your burden had been lifted from you? What made you feel that way?

Q: Do you believe Jesus paid for your sins by dying so that you do not have to perform different acts of penance or to gain indulgences? Explain your thoughts.

Q: In Psalm 51:16-17, David states, "You do not delight in sacrifice, or I would bring it; you do not take pleasure in burnt offerings. The sacrifices of God are a broken spirit; a broken and contrite heart." Is that how God sees you confessing your sins to Him?

Q: Tim discovered that God wants a contrite heart when we go to Him with our sins. In 2 Corinthians 7:10, Paul says, "Godly sorrow brings repentance that leads to salvation and leaves no regret, but worldly sorrow brings death. What does this verse mean to you?

Q: Are you taking advantage of Jesus' invitation to go directly to Him with your sins? _____ Take a few minutes and go to God now with your sins that you wrote down earlier. Earnestly and with a contrite heart, ask God for His forgiveness.

THINK ON THIS: John 5:22-23 "the father judges no one, but has entrusted all judgment to the Son, that all may honor the Son just as they honor the Father. He who does not honor the Son does not honor the Father, who sent him."

CHAPTER SIX

Saints As Our Intercessors

When you think of a saint, who comes to your mind first, Saint Joseph perhaps? Possibly the name of the grade school you attended, such as Saint Bernard or Saint Gabriel. In general, we all accepted Saint Nicholas as being real as we grew up. Many believe that Saint Nicholas, personified at Christmas as Santa Claus, was once a bishop who sailed around Europe and gave gifts to children; however, the spirit of Santa Claus is based on a much older mythical view of a father-like character who was capable of piloting a flying chariot and rewarding patrons with gifts once a year.

I have never prayed to Saint Nicholas, but I have written him many letters. As I deliberate on why my Catholic faith encouraged me to pray to the different saints, I looked into the church's definition of a saint. Next, examining the process of becoming a saint, and why only as a Catholic I could use saints as intermediaries—intercessors—to God.

Let us start by identifying what a saint is: someone who is recognized officially, especially by canonization, as being entitled to public veneration. That person is also capable of interceding for people on earth. A saint can be a person who is sanctified, a holy and/or godly person, one who is known for piety and virtue, any true Christian who has been redeemed and consecrated to God. Commonly, the term *saint* refers to someone who is exceptionally virtuous and holy. Sainthood can be applied to both the living and the dead and is an acceptable *term* in most of the world's popular religions. The saint is held up by the community as an example of someone who may model how we all should act, and his or her life story is usually recorded for the edification of future generations.

Saint Anthony, known for interceding by locating lost items, is one of the most popular saints. Any time you misplace your possessions, you have probably prayed to Saint Anthony for help. There are all sorts of popular medals with Saint Anthony's image stamped on them. You can even find outdoor statues of Saint Anthony holding the baby Jesus. Most Catholic religious stores carry holy cards and books on Saint Anthony. Different sites on the Internet even sell his medals. He has become one of the most beloved of Catholic saints.

You can also find many prayers to Saint Anthony on the Internet. One of the prayers reads, "Saint Anthony, perfect imitator of Jesus, who received from God the special power of restoring lost things, grant that I may find [mention your petition] which has been lost. At least restore to me peace and tranquility of mind, the loss of which has afflicted me even more than my material loss. Amen."

I doubt if you prayed those exact words. More than likely, it was probably something like, "Saint Anthony, help me find my keys that I have misplaced. I can't be late for my appointment." Frantically you continue to search around the house, letting out a joyous yelp when you found them in your pants pocket hanging in the closet. "Oh thank you, Saint Anthony," or maybe you muttered the words under your breath if you're alone.

Many parishioners probably called upon Saint Anthony once or twice in their lives. More than likely, you have had a conversation with a friend or family member explaining that you've lost your tickets or something else you desperately needed, and the reply to you was, "Just say a prayer to Saint Anthony, and you'll find what you're looking for."

Being encouraged to pray to the saints was part of my catechism experience. But I do not remember ever being taught when the church started proclaiming people as saints or how many saints that actually were proclaimed. I found this was a difficult question to answer; however, eventually I discovered a great answer from an article in the *Saint Anthony Messenger*, published in Cincinnati, Ohio, in the feature called "Ask the Wise Man." The article explained that in the first eight or nine centuries, there was no formal process for declaring someone a saint. People were recognized as saints by popular acclamation. Citizens were believed to be saints because they had been martyred for their faith or they had lived holy lives. Often their graves became places of pilgrimage and prayer. However, we have no idea of how many people's holiness went unrecognized. That is one reason why Catholics observe the Feast of All Saints. The celebration covers those who may not have been noted along with those who have.

The recognition of a person as a saint was of particular interest to a community because the reputation for sanctity spread beyond national borders. Patrons or the church from the town or area could make a lot of money selling relics of a departed individual. The first official canonization took place in the year 993. At that time, Pope John XV declared the Bishop Ulrich of Augsburg a Saint. The book *Butler's Lives of the Saints*, published between 1756 and 1759, listed names of 1,486 Saints. The 1956 edition contained 2,565 names. *Butler's Lives*, published by Liturgical Press, is now undergoing another revision. Because not all volumes of the newest edition have yet been published, I cannot tell you how many biographies or saints will be listed. In any case, I doubt that anyone will claim it is a complete and exhaustive listing of all the saints or people who are claimed to be Saints.

I had no idea there were so many who were proclaimed Saints. With that number of Saints, what was or is the procedure for achieving sainthood? First, we need to travel back in time to the tenth century, when Pope John XV authorized a special canonization procedure. The process took five years after the candidate's death. Bishops gathered to investigate the life of the candidate, and afterward the findings were sent to the Vatican. A panel made up of cardinals and theologians made the final approval. Afterward, the Pope proclaimed the candidate "Venerable," which means he or she was a role model of Roman Catholic virtues. The next step was beatification. The Church had to determine if the candidate was responsible for two proven miracles, which was performed after his or her death. Having proof of those two miracles, the designation of sainthood would be given. That procedure still remains today.

While understanding what a Saint was and the process of becoming a Saint, I found it particularly interesting that, contrary to the voting of the church leaders, nothing about the election of someone to sainthood or acting as an intermediary for God is found in the

Bible. Men who were designated by the church made the rules and declared the foundations of who and how one became a Saint. For the record, nothing indicates that the formation of sainthood was spiritually inspired, but the catechism of the Catholic Church states, "The communion of Saints is all the faithful of Christ, those who are pilgrims on earth now, the dead who are being purified, and the blessed in heaven, all together forming one Church."[1]

Here the Church is saying that all who belong to the Catholic Church are united as one unit. The church-going Catholics here on earth, including those who have died along with those waiting in purgatory and everyone who has gone to heaven, are universal. Because all are connected, a parishioner is able to call on them in prayer because they are united in the Catholic Church faith. This explains why I was encouraged to pray to them as a Catholic; however, what about all of those people who are not Catholic?

Many people question the true beliefs in praying to those whom men made into Saints. Therese Salzburg is one of those people. She was raised Catholic and was taught, as you and I were, that salvation is obtained by obeying the rules of the church. She said, "The Lord kept tugging at my heart that Catholicism wasn't right. One day I was at a Catholic Church listening to the priest explaining to a group of children to pray to saints for their different needs. How could he? Why did he not tell them the only way to the Father is through Jesus?"

Because of that encouragement from the priest to those children, Therese left the church at the age of thirty-nine, since the priest and the Catholic Church believe saints act as go-betweens. You may want to read the rest of her testimony at www.justforcatholics.org.[2]

As acknowledged earlier, the term saint refers to someone who is exceptionally virtuous and holy. Saints are held up by the Church as people to emulate. Following someone's good example of how to live is a good practice. Having a virtuous and positive role model is a good idea because he or she sets an example for all of us to follow. In declaring someone a Saint, however, the church officials have deliberately elected an intercessor–an intermediary—to God on my behalf. The Church has encouraged those of us who grew up Catholic, through its canons and the catechism, to pray to a deceased person who has been proclaimed a saint by a governing body of dignified men made up of priests, bishops, and

Popes. This belief in men electing saints began to trouble me a great deal.

In John 3:31, Paul says with extremely clarity, "The one who comes from above is above all; the one who is from the earth belongs to the earth, and speaks as one from the earth." Jesus never spoke of anyone from this earth as becoming a mediator for Him.

Christ wants us to go directly to Him, as He so clearly explains in John 14:6, when He says, "I am the way, and the truth, and the life. No one comes to the Father except through me."[3] I doubt it can be said any simpler than that. My belief of praying to the saints has changed because I, too, have said prayers to Saint Anthony many times as well as prayers to other saints. Accepting what I had been doing all of those years made me feel rather silly. Saint Anthony was an admirable man. He was an outstanding individual who had been honored in many ways for all the good he had done for the people and the church itself; nevertheless, praying to Saint Anthony or other men elected as Saints is wrong because of what Jesus says in Scripture. "God's doors are open to everyone. We all are God's creations, and He loves us so much that we are saints in His eyes when we have become united with Christ, but we elect to turn away from Him in the selfishness of sin."

I was overwhelmed when I recognized my prayers to the saints were nothing but words that I heard in my mind. In the true sense of tradition over the years, the church has elected countless people who allegedly are Saints who stand in the place of Jesus to answer our prayers. The Catechism of the Catholic Church explains the relationship with the saints this way: "Exactly as Christians' communion among our fellow pilgrims brings us closer to Christ, so our communion with the saints joins us to Christ."[4]

"By canonizing some of the faithful, i.e., by solemnly proclaiming that they practiced heroic virtue and lived in fidelity to God's grace, the Church recognizes the power of the Spirit of holiness within her and sustains the hope of believers by proposing the saints to them as models and intercessors."[5]

On May 13, 2005, Pope Benedict XVI opened the doors to allow Pope John Paul II to be named a Saint, only one month after his death. He lifted the rule that states a person must be dead for five years before he or she is able to have consideration of sainthood.

On March 31, 2007, a French nun who works as a nurse for the Little Sisters of the Catholic Maternities, is being sited as living proof John Paul performed a miracle after his death. Two years ago the nun, Sister-Marie–Simon Pierre was diagnosed with Parkinson's disease. After she and her friends had been praying to Pope John Paul she is now cured of that disease. As this book is being printed, the investigation is continuing as the Catholic Church passes a key mile stone in the drive to make Pope John Paul a saint.

Pope John Paul II removed the same rule after Mother Teresa died so she could be declared a Saint sooner. Once again, here are two wonderful people whom we all should look to as people to emulate. On the other hand, praying to Mother Teresa or to Pope John Paul II—if they are declared Saints by the church—is unnecessary in order to assist in my prayers being answered. I have someone who gave His life for me; He gave his life for you as well, and his name is Jesus. He ensures us that our prayers are heard. In searching for answers, I discovered that I can go directly to Him at anytime and any place.

We overlook the fact that Jesus' life is the one we need to emulate and make us want to live a better life by following His example and picking up our own crosses. The man-made saints, however, appear to be a better fit for us, perhaps it was because we could identify with them as being human. Each lived among us, worked among us, and probably had the same difficulties in life as we did. People also saw for themselves all the good they had done.

But didn't Christ live and work among the people in Israel? There can be no comparison to the good that He had done while on earth. He was the greatest who ever lived among us. But without hesitation we will pray to a person who has been declared a saint by a governing body who started the practice 993 years after Christ's death.

Seriously, look intently on the subject of declaring someone a Saint. My concern with sainthood: "Why would the church OK praying to men or women who have died instead of to the living God?" 1 John 4:9 NIV: teaches that Jesus was sent by God Himself. Each year we celebrate Christmas, which is the birth of Jesus, whom God sent to us. Remember John 3:16: " For God so loved the world that He gave His one and only Son, that whoever believes in Him shall not perish but have eternal life. For God did not send His Son into the world to condemn the world, but to *save the world through Him.*" Jesus confirmed that when He said, "No one comes to the Father except through me" (John 14:6). That is a powerful statement: we do not need to go elsewhere with our prayers. Jesus said to all of us, "All power is given unto me in heaven and in earth."[6] In John 5:22 are the words, "The Father judges no one, but has entrusted all judgment to His son, that all may honor the son just as they honor the Father."

People tend to honor the Church's power and not God's word when it comes to those difficult issues. Who are we to say someone is worthy of being a saint, then encourage the followers of the church to pray to those people that they elected to intercede for us? Ephesians 1:20 reads, "He exerted in Christ when he raised Him from the dead and seated Him at His right hand in the heavenly realms, far above all rule and authority, power and dominion, and every title that can be given, not only in the present age but also in the one to come."[7] Jesus reigns over all and has authority over all. He certainly needs no help from us on earth.

I found myself trying to dispute the truth that I was discovering and not wanting to withdraw from my Catholic traditions. But the overwhelming evidence that kept recurring in front of me of electing saints and praying to them was a man-made procedure. The question I pondered was, "Why Christ didn't share this with his apostles if it were so important?" Nevertheless, nothing is said or mentioned at all in scripture. Couldn't it possibly be that it is not important and we do not need an intercessor?

The bottom line on the subject of saints as intercessors is that God is continuously present for all of us. I discovered His hand is always reaching down to us. All we need is to realize this and reach out to grab on to it. As a Catholic, I was led to believe that praying to the saints brought me closer to God. Through all of the dogma that has been built up around this subject, I have justified that my prayers directly to God is what matters. He sent our intermediary: Jesus, His son. What better intercessor do I need? How do you feel?

Saints As Our Intercessors

SMALL GROUP OR CLASS LEADER: Review chapter five. As people arrive, ask them to write down the items they have prayed to Saint Anthony for, asking him to help find missing item's. Set aside a few minutes before the session ends so the group can write their own personal prayer to God in the last question.

Q: I prayed to Saint Anthony for:

Q: Did you have role model you emulated as a young adult? Why did you pick that particular person? Who would you pick today as your role model?

Q: When Therese Salzburg said that she overheard the priest explaining to a group of children to "pray to saints for their different needs," what was your reaction? Why do you feel this way?

Q: Why would the church OK praying to men or women who have died instead of the living God? What is your response to this question?

Q: In John 14:6, Jesus says, "I am the way and the truth and the life. No one comes to the Father except through me." Do you accept this as a certainty? Why or why not?

Q: 1 John 4:9 teaches that Jesus was sent to intercede for us by God Himself. Take a few moments and write out your own personal prayer to Him. Keeping in mind that He wants a relationship with you. Let your prayer be honest and from your heart.

CHAPTER SEVEN

Queen Of Heaven?

One of the most difficult roadblocks I encountered while searching for answers about my Catholic faith was coming to grips with the truth. Occasionally, the truth was disturbing, and often I had trouble accepting the reality of what I had learned. The evidence eventually became overwhelming. Surprisingly, I found myself part of that same evidence in the way I actually participated in what the Church approved.

A case in point is my belief about Mary, the mother of Jesus. In my effort to sort through and fully comprehend what I was taught along with what scripture says, I simply compared the Church's dogma to Scripture. The real vision of Mary started when I was a young boy visiting my grandparents one summer.

My grandparents were the greatest. I visited often and stayed through the weekend regularly. I even had my own bedroom that they had made up special for me in their basement. One summer weekend my grandfather was building a stone grotto in their backyard. The grotto was to contain a statue of Mary. I played a big part in the project, or so I determined I did as a six-year-old, by lending a hand mixing the concrete in the wheelbarrow and laying some of the small stones. The project was enormous and took three full, grueling days in the scorching sun to complete. The stone semicircle-shaped grotto stood about five feet tall when we finished. I remembered barely being able to touch the top of it, even when I stood on tiptoes.

The following weekend we went to the local nursery and chose some flowers to fill in the dirt area around the statue. The names of the flowers escape me; however, I remember how brightly colored they were. Pink, red, yellow, purple and blue flowers were carefully planted around the statue itself. Mary was made out of an incredibly dull grey concrete, so we spruced her up by painting the statue so that she had the typical blue and white veil. After making certain the finishing touches of paint were on the statue, my grandmother brought out a tray with thick sandwiches filled with ham and ice-cold lemonade for lunch. All three of us sat at the picnic table under the huge shade tree, with wide grins on our faces, admiring what we had built. I helped accomplish a major undertaking that summer. Not only did we achieve our goal, I realized my grandfather and I had become a team.

As a small boy, I recognized what we built was not something my grandparents would go outside and worship. The grotto of Mary simply represented a symbol of a mother who took care of her child, which happened to be Christ. As a member of the Catholic Church for many years, however, I as well as others elevated Mary to be more than a symbol. Mary was someone I prayed to. She acted as a petitioner for my prayers, similar to your asking your real life mother to intercede for you when you needed permission from your father for staying out one hour later than normal on a Friday night, for instance. You knew your mom could ask in your place and probably get permission. In the same way, I was doing the same when praying to Mary—asking her to lend me a hand in getting my prayers to Jesus answered.

Many consider Mary the pure channel to God. She is known as the holy mother, queen of heaven. When I was a child, my mother would recite the *Hail Mary* to us before we went to bed. I am sure you remember how it goes: *"Hail Mary, full of grace; the Lord is with thee, blessed art thou among women, and blessed is the fruit of thy womb, Jesus. Holy Mary, Mother of God, pray for us sinners, now and at the hour of our death. Amen."* Catholics and former Catholics are able to recite this prayer with no problem; once you learn it as a child, you never forget. During my journey to find answers, I learned that the Hail Mary was not a popular prayer before the eleventh century when the practice of reciting it began as part of the prayers of some monastic communities.

In the Church Council of 1198, Bishop Odo of Siliac required the clergy to ensure the faithful recited not only the *Our Father* and the *Catholic Creed*, but also the *Hail Mary*. Shortly after that, councils of many other countries made similar prescriptions, and the prayer became so popular that it was regarded merely as an appendix to the *Our Father*.[1]

Many people are able to tell stories and relate personal testimonies of Mary's interceding for them in their lives. Mary stands so high among us that she is also known to the church as the co-redemptrix. In other words, she works with Christ to save sinners.

Mary was the woman God chose to be the mother of His son, Jesus. We all are familiar with the story of the angel who visited Mary to give her the news. In Luke 1:30-32 NIV: the angel says, "Do not be afraid, Mary, you have found favor with God. You will be with child and give birth to a son, and you are to give him the name Jesus." Mary was truly blessed as she humbly accepted her role.

With all of her love and caring as a mother, she did not interfere with Jesus' ministry. Only one time did Mary step out and ask Jesus to perform a miracle by filling the water jars and making them into wine at the wedding in Cana. Aside from that, Mary played a low-key role throughout Jesus' three year ministry on earth. You could argue that the reason for Mary having this unassuming role was to assure that there would be no confusion of placing her on the same level as Jesus.

From personal experience, I know that most of us who grew up as Catholics elevated Mary in our hearts and minds. We "elevated" her to the point where it would offend us if we heard something contrary to how we felt about her. In fact, I found myself ignoring what naysayer's said about Mary. Remembering and examining carefully what I was taught, including my experiences in Church celebrating the *Assumption of Mary*, I could plainly see how the Catholic Church, and we as parishioners, have lifted Mary up, making her something she is not.

Dr. John Ankerberg and Dr. John Weldon successfully explain Mary's position on their web site, www.johnankerberg.org in the article entitled 'The Biblical, Catholic, and Occult View of Mary.'

"According to Rome, Mary has been blessed by God. In the words of Pope Paul VI, citing Vatican II. The place she occupies in the Church [is] 'the highest place and the closest to us after Jesus.' But according to Luke 11:27–28, Jesus Himself denied the Catholic leaders' views when He taught, 'those who obey God are actually far more blessed than Mary than if they had given birth to the Messiah Himself'. As Jesus was saying these things, a woman in the crowd called out, 'Blessed is the mother who gave you birth and nursed you.' He replied, 'Blessed rather are those who hear the word of God and obey it."[2] These are very powerful words that Jesus spoke about Mary.

Many of the prayers to Mary are called Marian Prayers and they include *Mary Immaculate, Consecration to Mary, Mary's Canticle—a hymn or chant—, The Memorare, and Hail Holy Queen,* to name a few.

In examining how we came to say the *Hail Mary* prayer, I discovered that the rosary was the most popular form of prayer in honor of Mary. The theory of the Church is that it had been given to us by Mary herself in the thirteenth century. The word *rosary* comes from the Latin word *rosarius,* meaning garland, much like a garland of flowers presented to Mary.

As I continued my search, I wanted to know the origin of the rosary, and why many people carried the beads, or actually wear it, as many priests and nuns have done and continue to do. Bear with me regarding the rosary for a minute. I think you will find this interesting. To my surprise, theologians have traced the origin of the rosary back to the ninth century as a form of prayer that evolved in the monasteries of the early Irish church. One of the most important forms of monastic prayer was the daily chanting in Latin of the 150 Psalms of David. Lay people around the monastery would hear the Psalms every day as they were sung or recited, and the beauty of those prayers intrigued them. They yearned to join in, but the Psalms were too long to memorize. Copies could not be found because printing was unknown before the late 15th century. Only a few knew how to read Latin.

Sometime around AD 800, the people's desire to participate led to their reciting the Lord's Prayer in response to every Psalm recited by the monks. As that form of devotion became popular, people began to carry leather pouches of 150 pebbles, so that they could keep count of their daily prayers when they were not in hearing distance of the monastery. A thin string with 150 knots became less of a burden and soon replaced the bag of stones. The Celtic infatuation with the number three soon saw the prayer string evolve into a string of 50 knots to be said three times, and that became an accepted standard.

During the thirteenth century, the recitation evolved into yet another form. Soon 150 praises in honor of Mary were also composed. In order to fit the existing prayer string, the praises were divided into three rosariums or bouquets of 50 each.

With the Church's emphasis on unity, it was inevitable that a combination of all the prayer forms was prescribed as a standard. The first step toward that standard took place about 1365, when Henry of Kalkar, Visitator of the Carthusian Order, divided the 150 salutations into decades of 10, with an *Our Father* preceding each. Around 1409, another Carthusian, named Dominic the Prussian, wrote a book that attached a psalter of fifty thoughts, about the lives of Jesus and Mary, to a rosarium of fifty *Hail Marys*. The division of the fifty *Hail Marys* into five groups of ten, or decades, with an *Our Father* before each, gave the modern rosary its form. Yet the evolution was not over.

In 1470, the Dominican, Alan of Rupe, founded the first Rosary Confraternity, thereby establishing the Dominican Order as the foremost missionaries of the rosary. During the Renaissance, the medieval form of a thought for each bead was abandoned in favor of a shorter version with a thought for each of the fifteen decades. Those thoughts took the form of narratives, one of the most popular sets of which was written by Saint Louis de Montfort around 1700. The fifteen narratives were divided into five Joyful, five Sorrowful, and five Glorious mysteries in the lives of Jesus and Mary, and the rosary itself became a string of fifty beads to be prayed three times, with each time representing one of the three sets of mysteries.[3]

My aunt had been detected with a mental disorder at a very early age and was unable to work a normal full-time job all of her life, but before she died of cancer, she handmade over 7,000 rosaries. They were all sent overseas to be given away. When I visited her in the hospital, she had one of her rosaries hanging on the hospital bedpost. The Rosary is a powerful prayer tool to many.

In the hearts and minds of many people, Mary is a spiritual mother to them and has made a huge impression. People will travel many miles to see her apparition. Crowds of people have been known to camp out for days just to place flowers at the site of where Mary was said to have appeared.

The National Geographic television channel aired a special documentary on July 31, 2006, called *"Ghosts,"* a program in which scientists investigate sightings of ghosts and apparitions. In the program, James Randi, a psychic investigator said, "We recognize facial impressions by instinct. A lot of times what we see is the result of misunderstanding of technology, psychology, or perfectly ordinary events that happen to us all the time."

In 2004, an image resembling the Virgin Mary was seen in the reflection of a building in Clearwater, Florida, during the daylight. "When the natural is easily explained, why go after the supernatural?" Randi asked.

On August 9, 2006, in the *Florida Sun Sentinel,* a headline read, "Pilgrims Say Water from Pope John Paul II is Holy." "People flocked to a new monument made to Pope John Paul II in his hometown and touched the water that ran over its base. They also collected the water in bottles in the belief that it carried healing powers. 'If the water comes from the papal monument, it is holy to us,' said Stanislaw, a thirty-seven-year-old electrician. One family traveled to see Pope John Paul's home where he grew up, but their first stop was the monument. Salwomir Poitrowski, forty-six, let the water flow over his hand before pressing it to his chest, convinced it will help cure his ailing heart. 'I am a little sick, and I am looking for strength to keep on going,' he said."[4]

People from across Europe and beyond came and washed their faces and hands in the cool, crystal-clear water that flowed over the dark granite. The mayor said, "The water was connected to the monument simply to enhance the granite's gray-brown color."

We need to be cautious about moving so quickly and clinging to what we want to pronounce a vision or a sign and reach out to embrace it as fact, positioning something we see as real before God Himself. I struggled, even as a Catholic, to see any truth in apparitions when the media reported people's sightings of Mary or events such as the water being holy from John Paul's statue. We are so hungry to clutch—something—anything—spiritual that we completely overlook the simplicity of hanging onto God's words and His teachings.

From my hospice experience as a chaplain along with the research on pre-death, I have discovered that about 80% of those people on their death bed do see loved ones who have died. These people also reported seeing spirit beings and angels at their bedside. One good resource on this subject is the book, "Into the Light" by Dr. John Lerma. I have been told many stories from family members that the patient would see their mother, father, friends including angels before they died. It is my understanding that they come to comfort us and help us cross over to the other side. Some of these sightings of loved ones would start as early as four weeks before the patient's death. This is far different from seeing a vision on a stained glass window or else where.

It seems that Jesus separated Himself apart from Mary. He indicated this in the following statements. In John 2:4, Jesus says, "Dear woman." He called her woman—not mother—although in those days, that phrase was not demeaning. He explains, "My time has not yet come." In John 14:6, Jesus explains again, "I am the way and the truth and the life. No one comes to the Father except through me." He never mentions anyone but Himself. Jesus is saying to us that He does not need Mary or anyone else as an intercessor for Him.

Here is a thought. As an adult, would you need or want your mother to be a go-between or intercessor for you? More than likely, no, and we are mere mortals. But we are talking about the Son of God Himself. Think for a moment: why would He need or want someone as a go-between? I get the impression that it's like an insult. For example, when Jesus prayed before his arrest He said, "And now Father, glorify me in your presence with the glory I had with you before the world began," John 17:5.[5]

"Before the world began" Jesus was and has forever been before Mary. God used Mary as a vessel for this earth. What an enormous and magnificent honor for Mary. What woman would not want to be a chosen carrier for God? However, I, too, needed to recognize that Mary was only a vessel. For many years, I neglected to not see her as she was intended by God, a selected vehicle for Christ. Acts 1:14 supports this: "They all joined together constantly in prayer, along with the women and Mary *the mother of Jesus*, and with his brothers." All of the apostles knew Mary as the mother of Jesus, not the mother of God, which I was taught. That latter concept is exceptionally difficult to accept. I needed to venture beyond

what I alleged to be acceptable based on my Catholic doctrine.

Three days after Jesus' death, He was raised from the dead. Jesus appeared to many of the disciples, but Mary was not mentioned as one of those He appeared to. We assume that Christ appeared to her, and it only seems natural for us to think He did, but it is certainly not mentioned anywhere. Naturally, Mary would want to share the news with the apostles or someone close to her if Christ had appeared to her. From the time Mary asked Jesus to fill the water jars with wine at the wedding in Cana, we know little about her. We know, however, that she was present at His crucifixion along with His brother John.

The next statement is an important moment in the belief in Mary as a divine individual, found in John 19:26 NIV: "Then Jesus looked down from the cross to Mary and said, 'Dear woman here is your son,' and to His brother John. 'This is your mother.' With those words of Jesus, the Catholic Church judges that at that moment Jesus declared Mary the spiritual mother of all members of the body of Christ." This is stated in the New American Catholic Bible published by Catholic Bible Publishers, 1985, edition.[6] Jesus only wanted his mother to be cared for, not worshiped.

Some believe that Mary has been elevated to her current position because the Church is so male dominated. If Mary occupies a superior position, then women worshipers will feel more included. Otherwise, women are largely excluded from the Church hierarchy, but there are no facts to prove this point.

As difficult as it may be to accept, Mary is not mentioned in the Bible as the one we should pray to or Queen of Heaven, nor did she have spiritual powers. In fact, Mary was a sinner as we all are. Paul says in Romans 3:10, "As it is written: there is no one righteous, not even one;" and in Romans 3:23 he says, "For all have sinned and fall short of the glory of God."

The Church and its veneration of Mary had been a way of life for me as a Catholic. We had statues of Mary inside and outside the church. I knew her as the Mother of the Church and the Queen of Heaven. But I found that to be untrue. And when we read in John 14:2 where Jesus says, "In my Father's house are many rooms," nowhere in that statement is Mary mentioned as queen of heaven in His Father's house. Nor does He say she shares His house. The term *Queen of Heaven* came from the Church hierarchy from their own interpretation of Mary. Jesus says, *"My Father's house"*—not anyone else's house—but His Father's. The last important element I looked at in regard to Mary was the Church's belief of raising Mary to be like a savior. Her assumption into heaven made her seem God-like to us. I was taught that Mary had been preserved free from sin, and it was not fitting that her body should undergo corruption. The new American Catholic Bible states, "It is also fitting that she should be the first of the redeemed to share completely in the victory of her son over sin and death. At her death, she was taken body and soul to heaven. She is the first human to share in the resurrection of Christ."[7] That privilege is known to us as the Assumption of Mary.

On May 1, 1946, Pope Pius XII asked all bishops in the world whether they thought the belief in the assumption of Mary into heaven should be defined as a proposition of faith. The majority of bishops replied that, yes, it should be. Later, on November 1, 1950, on the Feast of All Saints, Pope Pius XII declared the following: "From the universal agreement of the Church's ordinary teaching authority we have a certain and firm proof, demonstrating that the Blessed Virgin Mary's bodily assumption into heaven, which surely no faculty of the human mind could know by its own natural powers, as far as the heavenly glorification of the virginal body of the loving Mother of God is concerned, is a truth that has been revealed by God and consequently something that must be firmly and faithfully believed by all children of the Church."[8] Pope Pius XII proclaimed the Assumption of Mary to be true without any evidence. In the present day, on August 15 every year, the church celebrates the Feast of Mary's Assumption into heaven.

As I pointed out from my findings, it is stated by Catholic belief that Mary ascended into heaven without dying physically. When I saw what John says in John 3:13, "No one has ever gone into heaven except the one who came from heaven, the Son of Man," that was the final piece of proof that I needed.

For many, the proof of Mary not being the Queen of Heaven or having spiritual powers will not be accepted. Time may need to pass in order to acknowledge the truth because it is painful and contradictory to what we have been taught. The subject of Mary runs incredibly deep and personal; however, one must be careful and not take what tradition teaches to the point that the truth of what Jesus says does not matter. Some will choose not to abandon those traditions or customs, no matter what proof is laid out before them. What I found to be disturbing regarding Mary was that the Church's interpretation came before the teachings of the Bible. As a Catholic, one accepts the Church as the authentic moral and theological authority, which is our guide in interpreting the Bible.

I have reflected countless times on what Jesus and the apostles say in scripture. Even though I struggled with giving up what my faith had taught me all of those years about Mary, I had no problem determining whose words I needed to follow.

Being the mother of Jesus, Mary was truly blessed and a remarkable woman. She loved her son, mourned His death, and celebrated His resurrection. I do not want to downplay Marys importance in Jesus life, but if I were to accept Jesus for who He was, I needed to understand the truth of how the Catholic Church and I came to elevate Mary to be considered a spiritual mediator. Now that I have clearly found those answers, I am able to let go of the guilt I experienced and go directly to God. If God intended us to elevate Mary as a spiritual mediator Jesus would have told us through His teachings.

Please understand that I am in no way downgrading Mary's importance. Mary certainly played a very important part in Jesus life and could have been visited by Jesus after his death just as he visited the disciples. However, in the New Testament there were eleven sights recorded of Jesus during a period of forty days after his resurrection and none mention his mother Mary. I am simply stating that after doing my own research and asking sensitive questions and discovering the biblical answers I can go directly to Jesus with my prayers. I completely understand that I do not need to pray to Mary hoping she will take my prayers to Christ for me.

The more I reflected on what scripture says the more I realized that I needed to have an authentic relationship with Jesus all along. I must add that accepting Mary as a non-intercessor was not easy to accept in the beginning. Since childhood I had been taught to take my prayers to Mary, however, it was a huge break through knowing Jesus was just a prayer or a thought away. This unquestionably strengthened my personal relationship with him because I knew Jesus was approachable.

STUDY GUIDE QUESTIONS

CHAPTER SEVEN

Queen Of Heaven?

SMALL GROUP OR CLASS LEADER: Review chapter six.
This chapter completes section two. Check the progress of the group at this time. Make sure someone does not have a question or a comment regarding purgatory, confession, or the saints. Complete and discuss the following Questions.

Q: In what way do you know Mary? Was she the Mother of the Church and the Queen of Heaven for you?

Q: At some point in your life, did you consider Mary to be a pure channel to God? Explain why or why not. Has your answer changed in any way? If so, how is your answer different today?

Q: As a Catholic, Tim was taught that Mary ascended into heaven body and soul without dying physically. John 3:13 NIV, however, states, "No one has ascended into heaven but he who descended from heaven, the Son of man." Catholics and former Catholics have a difficult time letting go of that fabricated tradition. What is your view? Do you accept what scripture says?

Q: Is the statement in John 3:13 (above), all the proof you need to feel comfortable in taking a closer examination on how Mary is elevated and prayed to? Or does John's statement make you feel uncomfortable? Explain your thoughts.

Q: What does John 3:13 mean to you personally?

Q: Tim said, "We are so hungry to clutch—something—anything spiritual that we miss the simplicity of hanging on to God's words and His teachings." Do you agree with this statement? If so, do you find it happening in your own life at times? In what way?

Q: Tim also mentions that what he found to be disturbing regarding Mary was the Church's interpretation is placed ahead of the teachings of the Bible. Do you feel the same way? Explain your answer.

Q: Has this chapter brought you to a better understanding of Mary's role as Jesus' mother? Explain why or why not.

THINK ON THIS: Jesus came into our world and adopted our human nature to help us return to God. He identifies with us so that we can identify with Him. Oneness with Jesus brings us to oneness with God.

Obligated To Obey

"Modern American Catholics are divided over moral, social and political issues that have little to do with their faith in Jesus, and much to do with their personal histories and their own genetic codes," says Robert Blair Kaiser, author of *A Church in Search of Itself* (Knopf 2006).[1]

Disagreement mostly comes from how modern-day Catholics can live in a modern-day world and still feel comfortable about calling themselves Christians. With the Church's stance on second marriages, birth control and the increasing problem of people leaving the Church, we have only scratched the surface of what a current-day parishioner is willing to follow when it comes to the Church's governing beliefs.

Distorting, or hedging, by the parishioner is not uncommon when it comes to following Church doctrines. Parishioners may admire the Pope but do not take him too seriously on issues they disagree with. An Italian cardinal, Roberto Tucci, in an earlier stage in his career, was the Pope's chief trip planner. During one of his trips to America, someone asked Tucci what he thought about the relationship American Catholics had with the Pope, and his answer was, "I have the impression that they like the singer but not the song."[2]

As we transition into the rules and regulations that set the standard of beliefs a Catholic should follow and accept as true, the Council of Trent is a focal point, because it was the actual governing body that came together and arranged a central belief system for the whole Church to follow. This became another crucial step in determining whether I was going to give up my Catholic faith.

As I researched and made inquiries into the different canons and decrees, I found a true understanding of why I also was guilty of distorting or bending the rules as I practiced the Catholic faith. Although I am not proud of that fact, having belonged to a church that is governed by laws and traditions, I should have followed its teachings or not been a part of that organization.

My investigation produced some alarming results and created clear, concise answers regarding the Catholic doctrine and its beliefs through the canons at the Council of Trent compared to the Bible. If the normal churchgoer decided not to take the time to compare the two documents, he or she would not have been made aware of the major discrepancies. In the next two chapters, I will examine those differences in a practical, in-depth way.

Authority Of The Council

Many Catholic faithful never thought about or considered taking time to understand what the Council of Trent was about or what took place there. Like everyone else, I relied on the priest to inform me if there was a change in our doctrine. There were times when he would read letters from the archbishop or even from the Vatican encouraging us in different areas of our faith. That was the normal process for all of us. I went to church, followed the normal protocols and had no need to ask questions.

Growing older, I remembered hearing different comments about the Council of Trent, but my knowledge about it was limited at best. Not until later in life, when my world started falling apart, did I begin to start asking tough questions. I wanted to examine my own faith's bylaws. With many questions looming in my head regarding certain practices and beliefs, I strongly desired to understand the Council of Trent and why it played such a significant role in Catholic theology. After all, the decrees were the fundamental foundation of my belief.

I looked at the facts about the *History, the Objective and the Outcome of the Council,* along with how it affected what I was taught to believe as a parishioner.

The Council of Trent is the Nineteenth Ecumenical Council of the Roman Catholic Church, which was held from December 13, 1545, to December 4, 1563, in the city of Trent –modern Trento–, Italy, as a response to the theological and ecclesiological challenges of the Protestant Reformation. The Council is considered one of the most important councils in the history of the Catholic Church.

The Council clearly spelled out in detail the Catholic doctrines on salvation, the sacraments and the biblical canons. The Council standardized the Mass throughout the Church, largely by abolishing local variations. By doing so, that action brought everyone who was practicing the Catholic faith in line with the same teachings and beliefs. Different Catholic Churches could no longer practice the faith in the way they individually believed appropriate.

#1 The History of the Council of Trent

The history of the Council is divided into three general sessions: from 1545 to 1547, from 1551 to 1552, and from 1562 to 1563. The last was the most important. The number of attending members in the three periods varied considerably; however, attendance increased toward the close, but never reached the number of the first ecumenical council at Nicaea—318 members—, nor of the last Vatican—764 members. Two hundred and twenty-five members, including four papal legates, two cardinals, three patriarchs, twenty-five archbishops, and one hundred sixty eight bishops, with two thirds of them being Italians, signed the decrees.

2 The objective of the Council of Trent

The objective was to condemn the principles and doctrines that Protestants wanted to adopt and to define the doctrines of the Catholic Church on all disputed points. Simply stated, the Council's goal was to ensure that Protestant changes to the Church did not take place, including the Apocrypha. Protestants did not accept these additional books. They also disagreed with priestly celibacy, and did not believe in the transubstantiation or purgatory.

"It settled the burning questions of the rule of faith, original sin, and justification, in favor of the present Roman system and against the views of reformers...but it decidedly condemned the Protestant doctrines of the supremacy of the Bible, the slavery of the natural will, and justification by faith alone."[2]

Protestants, however, were invited to Trent to participate in the voting as a good gesture. They came and were prepared to vote on Church law but were denied a single vote by the Council. The Council wanted to ensure that only those who were practicing in the Catholic faith followed the Council's guidelines and its doctrine. Anyone who disagreed with any of the Catholic doctrines or canons it set into place were anathema to the Church.

We find one hundred and twenty-five anathemas in the canons that are doctrinal declarations of the Council. Those are found between two statements. The opening statement is, "If any man . . . . ," while the closing statement is "let him be anathema."[3] The Biblical Reference Guide of the New American Bible, published by Catholic Bible Publisher on page eight reads, "The term [anathema] was adopted by the church to express the exclusion of a sinner."[4] The word is used in Galatians 1:8 and I Corinthians 16:22 to denote separation from the Christian community, often used in the conclusion of creeds to condemn those who held incorrect beliefs; e.g., "If anyone should say that . . . let him be anathema."

Mary Ann Collins is a former nun who left the Catholic Church. She had entered the convent for several reasons. She said, "I wanted to be closer to God and to serve Him more wholeheartedly. I wanted to learn more about God and to spend my life being more intensely focused on Him. And I believed that God wanted me to be a nun."[5] Mary Ann gradually realized that some of the Catholic doctrines were contrary to scripture.

As stated, anyone who decided not to obey what was declared at the Council of Trent was to be cut off from the Church. The doctrines include the authority of the Pope, the practice of indulgences, the veneration of Mary and the saints, the use of statues and other sacred images, along with the belief that Jesus Christ is present in the consecrated bread and wine. The Council of Trent worded the Canon Laws in such a way that it expelled all Protestants because of their disbelief in what the Council declared was right.

The declarations and anathemas of the Council of Trent have never been revoked. All twenty-five sessions from the Council of Trent that explain the doctrinal declarations can be found at www. wayoflife.org/fbns/trent.htm."

I only include the fourth session here because of its significance. The length of the additional canons would not permit me to include them in this form. In the fourth session, it declared the additional books in the Bible to be acceptable. For me, why the Catholic Bible included those additional books and the Protestant Bible exempts them is vitally important to understand. If I were on the verge of giving up my faith, I needed to know why.

This is what I found. The Old Testament in Catholic Bibles

contains seven more books than are found in standard Bibles. Protestants call those additional books the Apocrypha, and Catholics also know them as the Deuterocanonical books. The seven books are Tobit, Judith, First and Second Maccabees, Wisdom of Solomon, Ecclesiastics (or Sirach), and Baruch. In addition, Catholic Bibles contain an additional six chapters in the book of Esther and another three in the book of Daniel.

The following decree deals with those additional seven books of the Catholic Bible. None of the Apocrypha claims inspiration or divine authority. The Protestant Old Testament omits several books, and when people speak of the Protestant Bible and how it differs from the Catholic Bible, this is the reason. The Roman Catholic Church formally canonized the Apocrypha on A.D. April 8, 1546, at the Council of Trent.

Fourth Session: Decree Concerning the Canonical Scriptures:

If anyone does not accept as sacred and canonical the aforesaid books in their entirety and with all their parts [the 66 books of the Bible plus seven apocryphal books, namely, Tobias, Judith, Wisdom, Ecclesiastics, Baruch, First and Second Maccabees and parts of Esther and Daniel] as they have been accustomed to be read in the Catholic Church and as they are contained in the old Latin Vulgate Edition, and knowingly and deliberately rejects the aforesaid traditions, LET HIM BE ANATHEMA.[6]

The Council of Trent makes it clear and accepts the additional twelve books that are not spiritually inspired.

#3 The outcome of the Council of Trent?

The Protestants' beliefs against the existence of the seven sacraments, transubstantiation, purgatory, the necessity of the priesthood and justification by works as well as by faith was successfully opposed. Clerical celibacy and monasticism were maintained, and decrees were issued in favor of the efficacy of relics, indulgences, and the veneration of the Virgin Mary and the saints. *Tradition was declared coequal to Scripture* as a source of spiritual knowledge, and the sole right of the church to interpret the Bible was asserted.[7] The last of these contributed to many of us not reading the Bible as we grew up as Catholics.

Both the Second Vatican Council —1962-1965— and the official

"Catechism of the Catholic Church"—1994—confirm the decrees of the Council of Trent and are still the Church's beliefs. When the Second Vatican Council began in 1962, Pope John XXIII said he accepted what the Council of Trent declares about justification and that any person who believes we are saved by faith alone is anathema. He also confirmed all past anathemas against false doctrine.

The modern Catholic Church can only be understood from the work that was done at the Council of Trent. The foundation on which those laws and the catechism of the Church had been instituted actually forced me to be cautious and investigate how I perceived the theology that made up and shaped my Catholic heritage. Those laws declare what the faithful can and cannot do. The canons define to whom Catholic followers should pray and in what they should have faith, which made me stand back and look at my core beliefs as a Catholic, including how I had been practicing my Catholicism all of those years.

I slowly came to the realization that the very foundation by which I was taught was very weak. I reflected on what I had discovered regarding the Council of Trent's decrees and canons and asked myself, if I were taught that Jesus was my only foundation from the beginning, and I did not need the man-made laws to follow but only the teachings of God, would I be searching and asking questions now about my faith? Hindsight is wonderful, but from what I have now experienced and witnessed, if I had learned Jesus' word through the Bible and realistically had a personal relationship with Him, my foundation unquestionably would have been stronger. And quite possibly, thousands more Catholics or former Catholics would not have to search for a solid belief structure to hold onto and feel secure in. No doubt, the Council had a major influence on all Catholics in how the faithful were directed to experience a relationship with God.

Lastly, in the area of religious doctrine, the Council refused any concessions to Protestants, and in the process, solidified and codified Catholic dogma far more than before. It appears that in the 16th century, the Catholic Church became more concerned about control, than enlightenment.

We all need a solid foundation in order to survive; however, man's interpretation of how that foundation should be built is capable of being flawed. Some who read this may feel offended believing that I am only showcasing the Council of Trent in a negative way in order to drive a wedge between current Catholics and the church itself. This is not my intention at all. I am merely expressing what I have learned so that as Catholics, the certain beliefs we followed may be clearly understood.

Authority Of The Council

SMALL GROUP OR CLASS LEADER: Review chapter seven.

Q: What did the Council of Trent accomplish?

Q: Does any one principle or tradition from the Council hold you captive? If yes, write those that do below.

Q: What does the word anathema mean?

Q: In 1962, at the Second Vatican, Pope John XXIII said he accepted what the Council of Trent declares about justification. It declared that any person who believes we are saved by faith alone is anathema. What is your view on this statement?

Q: In Ephesians 2:8 and 9 (New International Version), Paul says, "For it is by grace you have been saved, through faith and this not from yourselves, it is the gift of God, not by works so not one can boast." How would you compare Paul's statement to what the Council of Trent declared in the previous question?

Q: The canons define to whom we should pray and what we should believe. How does (or did) this affect the way you approach(ed) God?

Q: What is the difference between being religious and being a follower of Christ?

Q: Comment on the role the Council of Trent has played in your life as a former or current Catholic.

Q: As a group, read Colossians 2:8 as if it were a warning sign posted with bold letters for every follower of Christ to see. What is the content and purpose of this warning?

THINK ON THIS: Obey God, for God's goals are not our own. John 15:5 says, "I am the vine; you are the branches. If a man remains in me and I in him, he will bear much fruit; apart from me you can do nothing."

Catholic Doctrine Versus The Bible

I f you have ever traveled overnight on a business trip or taken
an extended vacation with your family, there is a good probability you have stayed in a hotel or a nice resort. As you unpacked
your belongings and proceeded to put them away, you may have
come across a Bible in one of the drawers. Bibles are in virtually
every hotel room in this country thanks to the Gideons, an evangeli-
cal organization founded over one hundred years ago. Annually, the
Gideons distribute more than 63 million scriptures worldwide.[1]

There are pocket Bibles, Bibles printed in all languages and Bibles
printed in extra large print. Bibles are available on the Internet and
recorded on CDs. Despite the easy access to the Bible, the majority
of us struggle to find time or simply do not take time to read it.

My grandmother gave my wife and me a large Catholic Bible as
a wedding present. As in most Catholic households, the Bible collected dust on a table; I never made an effort to open it. The Bible
was not part of our educational process when it came to church, and
reading it was not encouraged. I listened and learned what was in
the Bible on Sunday mornings when the priest read a few verses to
the congregation. If you were like me, you never personally picked
up a Bible to find answers or seek guidance. Even if I tried, I felt the
Bible was difficult to understand. My education about what was in
the Bible came from catechism, nuns, priests, and Catholic teachers
in school.

Catechism comes from the Greek word *katecheo*, which means
to "sound aloud." Catechism is a summary of Christian religious
doctrine. Catechisms are doctrinal manuals often in the form of

questions followed by answers to be memorized, a format that has been adopted for secular or non-religious use as well.

I have come a long way on my journey and discovered many truths, but it was critically important that I make a comprehensible distinction between what I was taught through my Catholic doctrine and how it compares to the Bible. By placing the two side by side, I could see a clear picture and easily identify the differences between them.

The following pages contain the Catholic doctrinal descriptions on salvation, grace, faith, and the basis for truth and idolatry, along with praying to those who are now deceased.[2] Each is absolute to Catholic beliefs. Following each Catholic description is what the Bible says about that particular subject.

Catholic Doctrine: Catechism of the Catholic Church (1994).

The Bible: God's Word in scripture.

• SALVATION BY GRACE ALONE •

Catholic Doctrine: Jesus sacrificed often.
"When the Church celebrates the Eucharist, she commemorates Christ's Passover, and it is made present. As often as the sacrifice of the Cross by which Christ has been sacrificed is celebrated on the altar, the word of our redemption is carried out." (380, Para.1364)

Every time that mystery is celebrated, 'the work of our redemption is carried on.' (393, Para. 1405)

Bible: Jesus sacrificed one time.
According to the Bible, our redemption to put away sin was a one-time act, which was completed at the cross, and it is said to be finished. "Now he [Jesus] has appeared once for all at the end of the ages to do away with sin by the sacrifice of himself." (Hebrews. 9:26)

"When He had received the drink, Jesus said, 'It is finished" (John 19:30) In whom we have redemption through his blood, the forgiveness of sins." (Colossians. 1:14)

Catholic Doctrine: Truth is based on scripture, tradition and the Pope.

"Sacred Tradition and Sacred Scripture are bound closely together and communicate one with the other." (*Catechism of the Catholic Church*, Para. 80).

". . . and [Holy] Tradition transmits in its entirety the Word of God which has been entrusted to the apostles by Christ the Lord and the Holy Spirit." (Para. 81)

"As a result the [Roman Catholic] Church does not derive her certainty about all revealed truths from the Scriptures alone. Both Scripture and Tradition must be accepted and honored with equal sentiments of devotion and reverence." (Para. 82)

"The Supreme Pontiff, in virtue of his office, possesses infallible teaching authority when, as supreme pastor and teacher of all the faithful, he proclaims with a definitive act that a doctrine of faith or morals is to be held as such." (Para. 891)

Bible: The Bible only is the Standard for Truth.

Jesus says, "the Scripture cannot be broken." (John 10:35)

"Sanctify them by the truth: Your word is truth;" (John 17:17)

"So that you may learn from us the meaning of the saying, 'Do not go beyond what is written'." (1 Corinthians 4:6)

"Do not add to his words, or he will rebuke you, and prove you a liar." (Proverbs 30:6)

"All scripture is God-breathed and is useful for teaching, rebuking, correcting and training in righteousness, so that the man of God may be thoroughly equipped for good work." (2 Timothy 3:16-17)

"Thus you nullify the word of God by your tradition that you have handed down. And you do many things like that." (Mark 7:13)

• SALVATION BY GRACE ALONE •

Catholic Doctrine: For salvation, grace becomes merely a help, and is given through the Sacraments of the Church.

"Grace is the help God gives us to respond to our vocation of becoming his adopted sons. It introduces us into the intimacy of the Trinitarian life." (Para. 20210)

"The Church affirms that for believers the sacraments of the New Covenant are necessary for salvation. Sacramental grace is the grace of the Holy Spirit, given by Christ and proper to each sacrament." (Para. 1129)

"One who desires to obtain reconciliation with God and with the Church, must confess to a priest all the unconfessed grave sins he remembers after having carefully examined his conscience." (Para. 1493)

Bible: Salvation is by Grace Alone through Faith.

"Being justified freely by His grace through the redemption that is in Christ Jesus." (Romans 3:24)

"For it is by grace you have been saved, through faith; and this not from yourselves. This is the gift of God: Not by works, so that no man should boast." (Ephesians 2:8-9)

"For if, by the trespass of the one man, death reigned through that one man, how much more will those who receive God's abundant provision of grace and of the gift of righteousness shall reign in life through the one man, Jesus Christ." (Romans 5:17)

He saved us, "Not because of righteous things we had done, but because of His mercy." (Titus 3:5)

"I do not set aside the grace of God, for if righteousness could be gained through the law, then Christ died for nothing!" (Galatians 2:21)

• FAITH IS GOD-GIVEN AND SUSTAINED •

Catholic Doctrine: Faith comes through the Mother Church

"It is the Church that believes first, and so bears, nourishes and sustains my faith." (Para. 168)

"Salvation comes from God alone; but because we receive the life of faith through the Church, she is our mother. . . " (Para. 169).

"Believing is an ecclesial act. The Church's faith precedes, engenders, supports and nourishes our faith. The Church is the mother of all believers. 'No one can have God as Father who does not have the Church as Mother.' (Para. 181)

Bible: Faith is the Gift of God and comes by the Word of God.
"Believe in the Lord Jesus Christ, and you will be saved, you and your household." (Acts 16:31)
"For it has been granted to you on behalf of Christ, not only to believe in him but also to suffer for Him." (Philippians 1:29)
"Consequently, faith comes from hearing the message, and the message is heard through the word of Christ." (Romans 10:17)

• GOD, THE ONLY ALL-HOLY ONE •

Catholic Doctrine: Mary is also the All-Holy One, and the Source of Holiness.
"By asking Mary to pray for us, we acknowledge ourselves to be poor sinners and we address ourselves to the 'Mother of Mercy,' the All Holy One." (Para. 2677)
"From the Roman Catholic Church he learns the example of holiness and recognizes its model and source in the all-holy Virgin Mary..." (Para. 2030).
"The Fathers of the Eastern tradition call the Mother of God 'the All-Holy'(Panagia), and celebrate her as 'free from any stain of sin, as though fashioned by the Holy Spirit and formed as a new creature.' " (Para. 493)

Bible: God is the Only All-Holy One, and the Only Source of Holiness.
"Holy, Holy, Holy, is the Lord Almighty; the whole earth is full of His glory." (Isaiah 6:3)
"Who will not fear you, O Lord, and bring glory to your name? For you alone are Holy. All nations will come and worship before you." (Revelation 15:4)
"There is no one holy like the Lord; there is no one beside you: There is no Rock like our God." (1 Samuel 2:2)
"I am the LORD; that is my name! I will not give my glory to another, or my praise to idols." (Isaiah 42:8)

Catholic Doctrine: In Salvation, Mary also mediates.

"Taken up to heaven she did not lay aside this saving office but by her manifold intercession continues to bring us the gifts of eternal salvation...Thus the Blessed Virgin is invoked in the [Roman Catholic] Church under the titles of Advocate, Helper, Benefactress, and Mediatrix." (Para. 969)

Bible: In Salvation the Lord Jesus Christ Alone Mediates.

"For there is one God and one mediator between God and men, the man Christ Jesus" (I Timothy 2:5).

Neither is there salvation in any other; "For there is no other name [Jesus Christ] under heaven given among men whereby we must be saved." (Acts 4:12)

• IDOLATRY •

Catholic Doctrine: The Roman Catholic Church Rationalizes Idolatry.

"The Christian veneration of images is not contrary to the first commandment which proscribes idols. Indeed, the honor rendered to an image passes to its prototype, and whoever venerates an image venerates the person portrayed in it." (Para. 2132)

"Basing itself on the mystery of the incarnate Word, the seventh ecumenical council at Nicaea (787) justified the veneration of icons—of Christ, but also of the Mother of God, the angels, and all the saints. By becoming incarnate, the Son of God introduced a new 'economy' of images." (Para. 2131)

Bible: God Hates Idolatry.

"You shall not make for yourself an idol in the form of anything in heaven above, or on the earth beneath or in the waters below. You shall not bow down to them, or worship them." (Exodus 20:4-5)

"He declared to you His covenant, the Ten Commandments; which he commanded you to follow and then wrote them on two stone tablets. You saw no form of any kind the day the LORD spoke so… that you do not become corrupt and make for yourselves an idol, an image of any shape, whether formed like a man or woman…." (Deuteronomy 4:13, 15-16)

"Dear children, keep yourselves from idols" (1 John 5:21).

• COMMUNION WITH THE DECEASED •

Catholic Doctrine: This Practice is recommended by Rome.

Communion with the deceased in full consciousness of this communion of the whole Mystical Body of Jesus Christ, the Church in its pilgrim members, from the earliest days of the Christian religion, has honored with great respect the memory of the dead. Our prayer for them is capable not only of helping them, "but also of making their intercession for us effective." (Para. 958)

The witnesses who have preceded us into the kingdom, especially those whom the Church recognizes as saints, share in the living tradition of prayer. Their intercession is their most exalted service. We can and should ask them to intercede for us and for the whole world." (Para. 2683)

Bible: This Practice is forbidden in the Bible.

"I am the LORD your God… You shall have no other gods before me." (Exodus 20:2-3)

"Let no one be found among you… who practices divination or sorcery, interprets omens, engages in witchcraft,… or who consults the dead." (Deuteronomy.18:10-11)

"I will set my face against the person who turns to mediums and spirits [divination; contacting the dead], to prostitute himself by following them, and I will cut him off from his people. Consecrate yourselves and be holy, because I am the LORD your God."(Leviticus 20:6-7)

This comparison of my education in the Church with the Bible teaching is purely straightforward and to the point. After deciphering each subject, I became aware that what I was taught growing up as a Catholic is not what God spelled out for me to follow. Understandably, some people will be offended by this assessment, but it was imperative that I look at each fact as stated. The reason this comparison is so essential is because the catechism of the Catholic Church is the foundation I grew up on and based my beliefs in. Until I'd seen this direct comparison myself, I would not have been able to make a definitive decision about my faith.

The assessment accomplished two things for me. One, it pointed out concrete facts leaving no questions as to what God expects of me. Two, it gave me permission to let go of my Catholic beliefs and establish a no-guilt conscience, resulting in no shame or regret for wanting to let go of the traditional teachings of my past and move forward.

By being so explicit and to the point, I honestly hope and pray you will not turn away, but instead pause for a moment and think about what you have read. I trust that this comparison will assist you in answering questions we as Catholics all tend to ask at some point, whether we like to admit it or not. You may be asking, was I taught the truth? Am I obligated to obey the Church's laws as stated because I am a Catholic? Should I pray to Mary and the saints? Do I believe that salvation comes by good deeds and works? Do I have faith in tradition over what the Bible says?

One of my aspirations when I started my journey was to discover the correct answers about my faith's foundation so I would be clear on the direction I needed to turn, and that I would have a meaningful life. In doing so, I discovered that if I forfeited what Jesus taught and accepted beliefs that were not His beliefs, I would be turning my back on Him. After all, what is one's existence without Jesus in your life?

For those who are searching, confused, frustrated, or not connecting with church, I implore you to inspect and evaluate your own situation, consider where your belief stands. Ask if that belief is solid, then examine how it influences your daily life. After years of hearing official dogma, I finally discovered what God had been trying to teach me through hard lessons in my own life. But sincerely believing that I already had a meaningful connection with Jesus, I was not willing to listen.

For more contrasts that are biblical, you can go to Richard Bennett's website at www.bereanbeacon.org. Richard is a former Irish Roman Catholic priest, who resides in the United States. He often speaks to different churches and organizations sharing his story.

CHAPTER NINE

Catholic Doctrine Versus The Bible

SMALL GROUP OR CLASS LEADER: Review chapter eight. Ask the group what they learned from comparing Catholic Doctrine to the Bible. Did any of the comparisons surprise anyone? What stands out most in your or their minds? Write down the answers and discuss as a group.

LEADER: Assign someone to read the following verses from John 1:1-3 and 14. "In the beginning was the Word, and the Word was with God, and the Word was God. He was with God in the beginning. Through him all things were made; without him nothing was made that has been made." Verse 14. "The Word became flesh and made his dwelling among us. We have seen his glory, the glory of the One and Only, who came from the Father, full of grace and truth."

Q: Ask the group what phrase in verse 14 tells us that the "word" refers to Jesus?

LEADER: Ask the following questions and encourage honest answers. No one needs to be embarrassed. Assist with the Bible challenge on the next page.

Q: How often do you read the Bible?

Q: How often do you go to the Bible to seek life's answers?

Q: How often do you search for guidance in the Bible?

If your answer to any of those questions was, "I do not own a Bible or I scarcely ever pick one up," this is a personal challenge for you starting tonight. Find your Bible and place it on the armrest of your favorite TV chair. *If you do not have a Bible*, all bookstores carry them. I suggest purchasing The NIV Study Bible, published by Zondervan. This one simple step is the basic fundamental building block to your journey of living life better.

Most of us have a daily routine in our lives. As Catholics or former Catholics, we were not exposed to a built-in routine that encouraged us to read the Bible, so consequently no routine was ever developed, and our spiritual growth curve has been greatly weakened.

Your challenge as an individual or class is to start a routine of reading the Bible every night before you leave your favorite TV chair for <u>five minutes.</u> Turn off the TV sit down and start with John in the New Testament. If you are using the *NIV Study Bible*, you will start on page 1591 in John, beginning with who the author was. After reading *John, go to Matthew where the New Testament begins.* Leave your Bible on the armrest of the chair so it will be there waiting for you the next evening.

IMPORTANT REMINDER: Bring your Bible to the next class session. The leader in the study class or small group should appoint someone to hold everyone accountable for bringing their Bibles to the next class.

THINK ON THIS: Obedience is the proof of our love for God. Read John 14:23-24.

The Heart Of The Mass

When attending mass on Sunday mornings, most consider it reverent and mystical. Walking into church, we dip our right hand in holy water, make the sign of the cross, and genuflect before sitting down. Serenity dominates the entire church atmosphere as people arrive to find their seats and wait for mass to begin.

With the many signs, symbols, priestly garments and actions that are present during the mass, it sends a signal of raw spirituality. At the center of the mass is the bread and wine which is turned into Jesus' body and blood. For that procedure to take place, the priest recites certain prayers along with the faithful, which is called the transubstantiation, i.e. the bread and wine are turned into the body and blood of Jesus at the altar.

Section Four investigates the significance behind the transubstantiation belief. Including resolving frequently asked questions that parishioners have about participating in communion at another faith-based church, such as, "Why does the Catholic Church seem to take communion more seriously than the Protestant church?" Or "I feel uncomfortable receiving communion if a priest is not present at the church I am currently attending."

I, too, felt strange, and had a difficult time participating in communion at another church. Feeling this way is the result of retaining several deeply embedded beliefs from our past, blocking us from accepting what Jesus intended for everyone. In chapter ten, as our journey continues, you will discover, as I did, what these obstacles are and the reasons why it is no longer necessary to embrace them.

A Meal To Remember

He took bread, gave thanks, broke it, gave it to them saying, "This is My body which is given for you; do this in remembrance of Me"

Luke 22:19

Going out to eat dinner is an occasion to relax, socialize and enjoy each other's company. In America, going out to eat with a friend or loved one is a social event, an excuse to get out of the normal routine of our hurried lives and enjoy the pleasurable opportunity it provides to unwind as we catch up with personal or daily proceedings.

If on a date, it is likely you would go to a restaurant for dinner, giving both of you a chance to talk or become acquainted in a pleasant surrounding. Around the table where there is food, thousands of dollars have been made from business deals conducted over lunch or dinner. In today's fast-paced commercial world, you meet business associates whenever and wherever it's convenient, including breakfast. It is a common practice. In fact, in Mexico between 8:00 a.m. and 11:00 a.m., business breakfasts are common. They take place in fine restaurants where business deals are firmed up or closed over a business breakfast.

If you have ever been on a cruise, there is a high probability you were seated at dinner with someone you never met before, although by the end of the voyage, you may have become good friends or, at the least, good acquaintances. You have learned how long your companions have been married, what they do for a living, all about their children and what part of the country they lived in. Maybe you've even exchanged emails to keep in touch after the cruise. When you think about it, coming around a table to share a meal with other people is a time for friends to gather, converse and share what you have in common.

For Catholics, going to church on Sunday mornings is similar. For example, receiving communion, *the bread and wine*, is the heart of the mass for the faithful. The sole reason for attending church on Sunday mornings is to receive the bread and wine as part of a group of people. This is also an important time at the Protestant church, although it is not the heart of the service.

The name of the service or assembly time in which the sacrament of the Holy Eucharist (eucharist is the Greek word for thanksgiving) is consecrated is called the liturgy or mass. In general, "liturgy" means a "work done for the Lord." For the Catholic church-goers Mass is formal and defined. The liturgy makes use of 1) readings from the Bible—the Word of God, 2) prayers based on the Bible, 3) spiritual songs, 4) sacred actions, signs or symbols including ceremonies and 5) extemporaneous prayers of the individual community.[1]

I sat down with my younger brother Michael, who had been a Roman Catholic priest for eight years, and asked him to explain, in his own words, the mass and why present-day Catholics in America go to church.

He said, "The celebration of the Eucharist, which focuses on the redemptive mysteries of Christ is the reason people go to Mass. To remember and celebrate Christ's saving actions as well as to draw strength to make Christ present and active in their daily lives. What happens within that hour is the community uniting around one big, Eucharistic table, identifying with one another and gaining strength toward leading positive Christian lives. The homily explains the readings from the Bible along with its historical and cultural significance. Using stories, current events and examples from human experiences, the priest tries to deliver a sermon that applies the scriptures to everyday life situations. The faithful are encouraged to identify with the message and live that message in their daily lives."

He went on to explain, "The mass, through the use of symbols, signs, words and actions, is a ritual that makes Christ present among the community. It builds up and sends forth the faithful into the world to be Christ for one another through actions of love and service."

After finishing with his answer, he gave me the impression that I'd made him quite nervous answering as if he recited from a text book: nevertheless, I continued with another question. I was curious to understand and get an unwavering, firsthand response about the transubstantiation, so I asked, "How would you describe the transubstantiation in your own words?"

He said, "Through the actions of the priest, accompanied by the prayers of the faithful, the substance of the bread and wine are consecrated and changed into the body and blood of Christ, while the appearances of bread and wine remain. The Eucharist is both a sacrament and a sacrifice. Jesus instituted the Eucharist at the Last Supper, giving thanks and sacrificing His life to God on our behalf. Through the sacrament of the Eucharist, He continues to communicate the graces merited to us on Calvary. The Eucharist is recognized as a community meal in which the participants know that the risen Lord is in their midst."

I asked, "Do you believe the bread and wine actually turn into Jesus' body and blood?"

"Yes I do," he said.

Although he is my brother and I respect him and his belief, Michael's answers did not correspond to what I learned from my research, and achieved nothing to change my apprehension regarding the transubstantiation. When I attended mass, however, at the point when the bread and wine were changed into Jesus' body and blood, I was to worship the Eucharist. The priest's changing the bread and wine into Jesus' body and blood was the reason, as a Catholic, I attended mass and received the Holy Communion from the priest. Having been taught that Jesus is re-represented by the bread and wine, which is being re-sacrificed for those who attend and receive communion, it was therefore crucial that we as faithful Catholics went to mass every Saturday or Sunday morning.

The act of the transubstantiation had been debatable in my mind for a long time. In high school, I began to consider the transubstantiation as only a symbol, not actually Christ being re-sacrificed, or His body and blood being the bread and wine at the altar. In believing this, however, I surprisingly discovered I had been sinning according to what the church teaches; when I attended mass on Sundays, I was sinning because I no longer accepted that the bread and wine were actually turned into Christ's body and blood right in front of me.

My quandary was that I received communion at mass, but because I did not believe in the transubstantiation, I was still sinning in the eyes of the Church. Discovering this disturbed me a great deal but I could not relate to the ability of a priest, bishop, cardinal, or even a Pope to turn bread and wine into the actual body and blood of Jesus. In my mind, they were merely men. How could such an act belong to any human? They were men, as I was, even though I held all of them in high regard as religious people.

I do not care to boast about this fact, but in my younger adult life I neglected mass on Sunday mornings and only attended occasionally. But in truth, I was not the only person missing mass for one reason or another, or who did not believe in the transubstantiation. As you can see from the article "The Ten Most Common Liturgical Abuses and Why They're Wrong" by Kevin Johnson, featured in This Rock magazine from Catholic Answers, only twenty-five percent of Americans who call themselves Catholic attend Mass regularly—down from seventy percent before the liturgical reforms following Vatican II. In addition, close to two-thirds of American Catholics say they do not believe in the true presence of Christ in the Eucharist, and many of those are among the twenty-five percent who still attend Mass today."[2]

I discovered that I had been sinning on two fronts according to the Church. One, I choose not to attend mass every Sunday. Two, I did not agree with the transubstantiation. My heart sank thinking of all of those people who may be in this same situation but are unaware of it.

I had been caught in a vicious circle, but not cognizant of that fact until I did my research. Not going to a priest for penance was considered sinning, because I was not practicing the sacrament of penance, in turn I was not allowed to receive communion for that reason. I was also sinning by Church's doctrine because I did not believe in the transubstantiation but received communion anyway. This raised two major concerns for me: first, what are the existing Catholic faithful doing if they do not believe in the transubstantiation and still receive communion? Second, what are former Catholics doing about receiving communion if they are attending a Protestant church?

Don't worry, if you are one of the Catholic faithful who was unaware that you are sinning because you did not believe in the transubstantiation, by church law you have not sinned yet because you simply were not knowledgeable of this fact. However, now that you are aware, take time and examine what you do and do not believe. I found all the dogma became increasingly confusing. You may need to consider if you will go to confession or continue to receive communion. These and many other questions you will need to answer for yourself.

For the former Catholics who are currently attending a Protestant church and acted as I did, by not accepting communion at service because a priest was not present; the question I want to address is, "Why are we former Catholics so hung up on not taking communion when attending another church?" I believe that we are missing the whole point by being misinformed.

I, too, at one time, was apprehensive when the communion tray came around to me as I attended Northeast Christian Church. My wife would hand me the bread and juice tray and without hesitating for a moment, I quickly passed it on to the next person. I had no intention of participating in a Protestant communion. I had been dwelling in the past, unwilling to let go of the tradition ingrained in me. Although that strong defiance made me feel embarrassed, not wanting anyone to notice I was not participating.

After several weeks of attending church and passing along the communion tray, Genora finally asked point-blank, "Why do you pass on the communion tray and not participate?"

Not wanting to admit that I was still hanging onto the rituals and my inner feelings of being a Catholic, I said simply, "It doesn't feel the same."

The following Sunday, as I passed the communion tray to the person next to me, I began to wonder if my pride of being a Catholic was the real reason for my not taking communion. I sat and thought to myself, *if I did not consider the true presence of Christ was in the Eucharist itself, then why would I not go ahead and receive communion at a Protestant church?* What was holding me back? Struggling with all of the dogma from my background, the teachings and beliefs I grew up with continued to have a tight grip on me. Having something so influential with me since a few weeks after birth is tremendously difficult to let go of; however, I was not alone in my feelings or actions.

After hearing from many people who came from the Catholic background, their reactions were similar to mine about receiving communion at a Protestant church.

I decided to dig a little deeper to find the reason behind my actions, partly because I was so embarrassed of passing the tray every week without partaking. Humbling myself, I finally asked for help and learned there is no place in the Bible that states a priest needs to be present for us to receive communion. Learning this, I wondered what I was trying to prove to myself. Could it be that I was afraid of breaking away from the norms of Catholicism, where a Catholic may celebrate communion, reconciliation, and anointing of the sick only from a priest and only in whose church those sacraments are valid? But the heritage and laws I'd tried to follow since birth subconsciously would not permit me to let go of them.

Things did change, however, with the guidance of Bob Cherry when he encouraged me simply to read the Bible and ask questions. I was able to find the answers regarding communion at a Protestant church service. As I stated earlier, Jesus said, "This is my body given for you: Do this in remembrance of me." *"Do this in remembrance of me"* is the key phrase here. Christ explains that each time I receive communion, I am to remember that He died for my sins. For that reason, the real question is, why not participate in communion at a Protestant church, if by doing so I am remembering His death? This would be the most obvious consideration toward Jesus I could perform. The answer had become much clearer to me, and making excuses such as, "Without the priest being present, it is not the same," or, "The small pieces of hard bread look nothing like the rounded hosts I used," undoubtedly no longer applied.

The bread and wine at the Last Supper—which we call communion—is a symbol to remember what Jesus did on the cross. He wanted us to remember Him, whether the bread we ate was small, large, round, or square. When we drink the communion cup, wine does not need to be involved. Juice, water, or even lemonade would be fine. Do not miss Jesus' point of remembering Him by the justification of the exact emblems. What good is receiving communion if you fail to remember Jesus on the cross, as He asked?

I don't mean to go too deep with this but what is important is that communion is remembering His selfless act of dying for each one of us, a self-sacrificing act of love, which none of us truly deserves. Participating in communion—no matter where we attend church—is a solemn and personal time for all of us to go to Jesus for remembrance, reflection and giving thanks for His grace.

I found that the Protestant church does bring reverence to communion time in different ways, by the words on the video screens (if they are present), by the soothing reflective music, or the silence. But far more important, it is those people who are actually receiving communion and doing what Jesus had asked that brings reverence to communion. Remembering His death, silently telling God how we feel and where we have failed Him. During this time, people reflect and pray. Communion is more than a life audit; here we seek a true spiritual union with God.

I was not shocked by some of the statements people made in the "Growing up Catholic" classes. I related exactly to what the participants were saying. I heard comments such as, "Communion did not seem as spiritual in a Protestant church to me," or, "The Protestant church does not regard communion as seriously as we do in the Catholic Church," and, "The reverence of the service is not there for me at a Protestant church."

True, differences cannot be overlooked at a Protestant church. Ever since I could remember, the Catholic priest wore brightly colored garments on Sunday that made him look reverent. In addition, the mysticism that surrounded the mass itself created a sense of deep spiritual awareness.

As for the Protestant church not taking communion seriously, we as Catholics had so many rituals to follow, it blinded our thinking to the point of believing that the Protestant church was not serious about communion. As an example, we saw lit candles and holy water as we entered the church. Statues of Mary and Joseph stood in view, and we identify with them, along with colorful stained-glass windows, as the sharp smell of incense filled the inside of the church.

We received communion from the priest in specific ways. If you remember in the early days, we never touched the host ourselves. We walked up to the priest who placed the host on our tongue for us. We were taught that God's gift is something that we receive, not something we reach out and grab. The altar boy or girl held the gold round disk under our chin; if the host fell, it could not land on the floor because it was actually the body of Christ. Tradition has changed a great deal; now we are able to remove the host with our own hand as the priest places it in our palm; then we pick the host up, placing it into our own mouth.

All of the rites, gestures, rituals, the burning of incense and reverence have a tendency to make a person imagine that taking communion at a Protestant church is not sacred; this is completely false thinking on our part. No doubt, by attending a Protestant church things are different; however, communion is a reverent time at a Protestant church, in spite of the bread's looking different and people not getting up from their seats to receive communion from a priest. But there are times in Protestant churches when the communicants get up to receive the bread and drink from a cup of juice or wine. If you open your mind to God's teachings and truly listen, the answers about taking communion at another church will come unmistakably. You will know in your heart what is right. The Catholic Church and Protestant churches actually have many beliefs in common.

The next time you are sitting in church thinking about passing up the communion tray because it is not a Catholic mass, contemplate the things that both faiths believe in:

1. God is the creator of heaven and earth.
2. The purpose of life is to know and love God.
3. Jesus is the Lord and Savior.
4. The Bible is the inspired word of God.
5. The Trinity is the Father, Son, and Holy Spirit.
6. God became human in Jesus through the incarnation.
7. Grace is necessary for salvation.
8. Jesus asked all of us to remember His death on the cross by taking bread as a symbol of His body, and taking the juice—or wine—as the symbol of His blood.

The laity is responsible for knowing the laws about texts, gestures, the sacred objects used and the proper conduct of the mass, obeying those laws and seeing that the clergy obey them, too. I found myself asking which laws—God's law or man's law?

When answering this question, it became obvious to me that we only need God's word and God's law, not the laws of theologians.

This includes the correct way to receive communion and remember Jesus' death on the cross. The colorful garments, the holy water, the statues, the gestures, and so on are insignificant and unnecessary when making a decision at another church to receive communion and remember what Jesus did.

The decision I had to make at a Protestant church centered on the understanding that it was not my surroundings or my personal feelings of how I perceived communion should be. Knowing Christ loved me enough to die for me and not hold me accountable for a ritual, but instead, hold me accountable for remembering His death made the difference in my backward thinking.

Believing I could not participate in communion because I was not in a familiar surrounding where I was expected to follow particular procedures was exceedingly selfish of me. Communion is between a person and God. When we brought man into the picture, it clouded our union with Him. What is stopping you from gaining so much by participating in a merger with Christ the next time you receive the communion tray at church?

STUDY GUIDE QUESTIONS

A Meal To Remember

SMALL GROUP OR CLASS LEADER: Review chapter nine. Chapter ten starts section four. Check on the group's progress to this point. Ask how many in the group remembered to bring their Bibles this week. Those who have one, share with those who do not. Ask everyone to turn to 1 Thessalonians 2:13 (New International Version). Assist in finding the Bible verses below.

Q. Because the Bible is the word of God, you can believe what it says. 1 Thessalonians 2:13: what does the phrase "You accepted it not as the word of men" mean to you?

Q. Now turn to 1 Corinthians 11:23-25. Do you see any stipulations that would make you believe Christ preferred that you took communion in a certain surrounding or with particular emblems?

Describe below your thoughts on what you have just read.

Q. If you are currently attending a Protestant church, do you participate in communion? If not, explain what may be holding you back. If yes, did you hesitate in the beginning and were you uncomfortable? Explain.

Q. By reading the same verse above, do you feel a priest must be present in order for you to receive communion? If yes or no, please explain your answer below.

Q. As a symbol of His death, communion allows us to remember Him. When Jesus said, "This is my body given for you: Do this in remembrance of me," what is Jesus saying to you personally?

Q. Were you aware that not believing in the transubstantiation and continuing to receive communion was considered a sin in the Catholic Church's eyes? Knowing this, will it affect the way you receive communion at the Catholic Church if you are currently attending one? Explain why you feel this way.

Q. Will the decision that you make to receive communion at a Protestant church ultimately be centered on the surroundings that you grew up with and your personal feelings of how communion should be preformed or represented, or will it be simply because Jesus asked you to remember His death, no matter where or how you receive communion? What are your thoughts?

Q. "Communion is between you and God. When we brought man into the picture, it clouded our union with Him." Do you agree with this statement? Explain what the phrase "it clouded our union with Him" mean to you.

THINK ON THIS: John 5:24, "I tell you the truth, whoever hears my word and believes him who sent me has eternal life and will not be condemned; he has crossed over from death to life."

A Radical Discovery

The previous chapters asked powerful, straightforward, hard-hitting questions about purgatory, confession, Mary, communion, and the Catholic doctrines. I finally found and faced the real reason behind the void—emptiness—within me. Soon my journey would bring me face to face with the decision of actually doing something about it.

Through the difficult process of having questions answered regarding my faith, I discovered I could not get to God unless I got to Christ. In the beginning, I was boldly under the false impression of having a real relationship with Him. Not until I learned that the most important priorities in life were God, family, friends, church, and work, exactly in that order, did I begin to understand what a real adventure and personal relationship with Jesus is. All too often, we think life is all about me. Our culture relentlessly promotes and bombards us with a drive to fulfill our own self-needs daily, even to the point of our becoming addicted to harmful behaviors. Until we realize that life is so much more than self-righteousness and self-fulfillment, we will continue to struggle to find a better way to live.

One frequently asked question, which turns into many irritating questions, is, "Why do I have to be re-baptized if I have already been baptized as an infant?" "Wasn't the first time good enough?" or, "Are you trying to tell me my baptism was wrong and not done properly?" This is an emotional and heart-wrenching question we often find ourselves debating. More times than not we let our emotions get away from us as anger and resentment come to the forefront because we are frustrated that someone even suggested it to us. Sometimes to the point of leaving a church we have been visiting. Many former Catholics understandably do not wish to discuss the subject of re-baptism. As a Catholic, when you heard the question, you may have felt as if your spiritual life has not been good enough, you take it very personally and it deeply affects you. Hurting, you become defensive and you start to build that invisible brick wall around you. You can now feel somewhat protected because your pride and your feelings are intact. But be assured that you are not alone in building that brick wall, it is extremely common to feel as if you have been violated. I too felt this hurt; it damaged my pride and annoyed me.

I know Jesus has come for all people, including me. I wanted to have an authentic connection with Him by learning how to live my life depending on Christ for wisdom and guidance, instead of solely depending on myself.

Now that I had the answers, it was time to take action. The next three chapters disclose how I came to understand and value Jesus in ways I could not have ever imagined by accepting Him into my life; moreover, I had no idea what was in store for me.

I Have A Decision To Make

If you are Catholic, it is highly probable your parents were baptized as infants. Their parents and our parents acquired the responsibility of raising us in the Catholic Church. They boldly stood as our representatives for the sacrament of baptism, as is expected. They followed their heritage along with the traditions of Catholicism and formal procedures they were taught growing up. Sadly, that enormous event—the sacrament of baptism—does not register in our mind as adults, nor does the baptism of our parents register in their minds.

Please do not misunderstand what I am saying. I am grateful for the love and care my parents gave me through those years of raising me. They implemented what all Catholic parents elect to do and decided it was best for me to be baptized as an infant by following the Church's traditions.

My only responsibility as an infant was to eat and sleep. I depended on my parents to care for my every need—everything— even telling God that I would be brought up Catholic, obeying the Church's teachings precisely as they did. My mother and father were simply following what the Catholic catechism taught them and their parents, for generations.

Why did our parents elect to baptize us as infants? As Catholics, they understood baptism to be regenerative. In other words, it removed the stain of original sin and infused sanctifying grace into the soul. Therefore, what Catholic parent would not elect to have their baby baptized? This was an enormous responsibility our parents took on in making that heartfelt decision. However, I was never personally asked to make the commitment for myself or make it from my heart. Had I been asked, this would have given me the opportunity to engage in the seriousness of my decision and take responsibility for the commitment I would be making by learning how to grow spiritually in Christ. But in its place, I grew up with a foundation built by the tradition of receiving the sacraments needed for salvation, as the Church states. As a result, my walk with Christ was a casual one at best, although I believed otherwise, which resulted in me taking charge of my life on my own terms, in my own way.

Baptism by immersion is a subject we can beat to death as we analyze it repeatedly. The subject of baptism, unfortunately, has divided faiths, marriages, families, and friends. When it comes to explaining why one person feels they need to be sprinkled as an infant and one needs to be immersed, we all too often find the battle lines are drawn and trenches dug for war. I went through the same battle. I wondered what God thought when we argued over which was correct. Were we more concerned about what God wanted or about what we wanted?

I simply wondered how our parents or the Church could possibly be wrong in deciding what God wanted for us. This initially played a vital part in my thinking each time someone mentioned baptism by immersion. Deep down, I unequivocally understood I was a Catholic, which meant having deep roots to my faith.

By evaluating my experiences and coming to my own conclusion about baptism, I needed to be stern about finding the truth concerning being re-baptized as an adult. I took on the responsibility of being completely open to what Jesus said and taught about baptism, which included evaluating what the Catholic doctrine expected of me. I examined in detail what the Bible said on the subject of baptism. I sought to set aside my personal arrogance of what the Church had taught me and evaluate what I should do. This was not an easy task to accomplish.

My Catholic friends explained to me that being re-baptized as an adult was not necessary for salvation. "You were already baptized as an infant," they would explain. Their words only increased my desire to scrutinize the question of me being re-baptized by immersion. As I looked at the facts according to the Catholic Church, there are three main sacraments necessary for justification and ultimate salvation. Those sacraments supposedly communicate grace to an individual and help to maintain a Catholic in a state of sanctifying grace. They are baptism, penance and the Eucharist (the mass). Remember, sins committed after baptism must be dealt with through the sacraments of penance and the mass itself.

In order to regain that state of grace with God, the individual must participate in those sacraments because the atonement of Christ was not the exclusive cause of man's redemption. For Catholics, a person must supplement the work of Christ for sins committed after baptism by partially atoning and expiating his own sin through penance. If I were to be re-baptized in a Protestant church, I would no longer be following those sacraments for salvation, as I knew them. I only wanted to follow what was right in God's eyes by following what Jesus said in scripture.

I ask that you bear with me for a moment, one more time. It is important I address the belief, "it's all in how you interpret the Bible" at this point. Some may not accept the Bible is from God. Earlier in my life, I had a difficult time believing everything written in the Bible was true. I have met people who defended their interpretation of the Bible by explaining, "The truth in the Bible is how a person may interpret it himself." They would say, "I only accept particular parts of scripture to be true, but not everything."

We certainly can believe what the Bible says, not only because it is God-inspired and Jesus' living testimony, but also because the word *testament* comes from the Latin word *testamentum*, which means *covenant*. The Bible is a covenant—a promise or contract—a document spiritually inspired by God. John 10:35 states, "The scripture cannot be broken." In addition, in 2 Timothy 3:16, Paul says, "All scripture is God-breathed and is useful for teaching, correcting, and training in righteousness." In the *Encarta Dictionary*, the word *gospel* is defined as, "something believed to be absolutely and unquestionably true." The New Testament is a message given by those who knew Jesus personally or had been spiritually impacted by Him. 1 Corinthians 15:1-2 is an example of that message. "Now, brothers, I want to remind you of the gospel I preached to you, which you received and on which you have taken your stand. By this gospel, you are saved, if you hold firmly to the word I preached to you. Otherwise, you have believed in vain."[1]

I understood with clarity what is written in the Bible to be true and capable of saving us if we would adhere to its teachings. I needed no proof that Jesus was sent by God to show us the way but on the other hand, being Catholic, I had never been exposed to the in-depth detail of the Bible before. I am certain there are many others like me who are in the same predicament when it comes to the details of scripture.

Now that I addressed, "It's only how you interpret the Bible," it will be much easier for you to understand why I took what scripture said seriously. When I contemplated being re-baptized, as an adult by immersion, the most serious explanation I took into account was what scripture said and what Jesus actually did Himself. In Matthew 3:13-17, he tells us that Jesus came to John at the Jordan River to be baptized by him and at that time, Jesus was thirty years old. After Jesus received the baptism from John the Baptist, He came up from beneath the water. God said He was pleased with what Jesus had done. A voice came from heaven, saying, "This is My beloved Son, in whom I am well pleased."[2]

Coming to understand what I read in the Bible and the act of Jesus Himself being baptized by immersion (beneath the water), the pride I carried with me of being Catholic soon started to change to one who was humbled. The defensive barrier I set into place regarding my faith started to break down. I asked myself, "Am I simply too engrossed in my own beliefs, or perhaps too stubborn to listen to what the scripture was saying when it came to baptism?" Should I be baptized by immersion, exactly as Jesus was?" The Bible even gives proof of eyewitnesses. *What was my problem with being re-baptized*, I kept thinking to myself.

I started to approach it in a different way. If I could be baptized as an infant, not even remembering the event, surely as an adult I could personally and physically show Him I believe in His word and accept this responsibility by following His teachings by being re-baptized. I kept repeating the same question—what is the problem with baptism by immersion as an adult?

Still the question was eating away at me and I needed absolute understanding. So I asked, "What was the symbolism of being immersed, and what did it mean anyway?" I found that being baptized by immersion was the symbol of dying to one's old self, washing away sins and being born to a new self. This is the source of the term "born again" and signifies the start of a new journey in one's life, a commitment to follow Christ.

I went so far as to ask myself why Jesus needed to receive a baptism in the first place. I read the reason in Matthew 3:15. It was to fulfill all the righteousness of God: "Permit it to be so now, for thus it is fitting for us to fulfill all righteousness". Here, "to fulfill all righteousness" refers to fulfilling God's love toward us, the sinners. Simply put, in order to deliver all sinners from their sins, Jesus came into this world and received the baptism from John the Baptist. Through His baptism in the Jordan River, Jesus took onto himself all sins of humanity. Then He had to shed His blood on the cross to pay off all the sins He had taken on with His baptism.

It is better explained in Romans 6:3-7. "Or don't you know that all of us who were baptized into Christ Jesus were baptized into his death? We were therefore buried with him through baptism into death in order that, just as Christ was raised from the dead through the glory of the father, we too may live a new life. If we have been united with him like this in his death, we will certainly also be united with him in his resurrection. For we know that our old self was crucified with him so that the body of sin might be done away with, that we should no longer be slaves to sin because anyone who has died has been freed from sin".

The New Testament does not contain explicit written instructions on how to actually perform a baptism. As we have read, there are verses describing how Jesus and others went into the water. In fact, the word *baptize* comes from the Greek word *baptizo* which means to "place in or immerse" as in physical immersion found in the New Testament. Jesus was explicit in showing us the example Himself by going into the water to meet John in the river to be baptized.

I understand many devout Catholics will continue to argue that the testimony of the Diache is a true explanation of how to baptize. The Diache was written around A.D. 70; though not spiritually inspired, it circulated among the churches in the first few centuries directing, "Baptize in living water—that is, in running water, as in a river. If there is no living water, baptize in other water, and if you are not able to use cold water, use warm. If you have neither, pour water three times upon the head in the name of the Father, Son and Holy Spirit."[3]

The above gives three ways to baptize with the first being in somewhat deep water. By following Christ and believing his word in scripture, if it was physically possible for me to be baptized by immersion and not hindered by any bodily problems or severe illnesses that kept me from doing so, then I needed to follow His example by showing Christ I honestly believe in His teachings. I understood and accepted that I was truly lost before—although I thought otherwise—because I was illiterate of the Bible. Being conscious, of what I did not know before, the Bible opened my eyes, helping me to understand clearly the decision I was about to make, quite the opposite of when I was an infant. The truth of the matter is Jesus gave the illustration for us to follow by being immersed Himself.

With one last concern on my mind regarding baptism, I sat alone at home one evening wondering, how much faith is needed to receive Jesus? I considered myself a "back-row Joe" type of person, so would someone like me have enough faith?

Finding the answer was a relatively simple task. John Ankerberg, writes in an article on his web site at www.johnankerberg.com on *How to Become a Christian*, explaining the answer this way: "Realize that in one sense, it is not the amount of faith that saves you— it is *in whom* you put your faith." The question you should ask, "Is the Savior strong enough and dependable enough to save me when I ask?"[4] When it came time to make my decision about the foundation I grew up on, regarding being re-baptized, that foundation no longer had support. After battling over the Catholic beliefs and listening to other people give their opinions, it all came down to what Jesus asked us to do, which was to surrender how I dictated my own life and follow His way of living. For that reason, I would not allow anything to keep me from becoming part of the death and resurrection of Jesus by not being re-baptized by immersion.

I now understood completely the purpose of being re-baptized, but many of us go back and forth, pondering what we should do. I was a perfect example. The following is the true story of one Catholic family who struggled with being re-baptized by immersion as adults.

Tim and Angie Hollinden, at the time both forty years old, had two children–TJ, twenty and Terra, eighteen. Angie went through the difficulties and stresses of explaining to her parents her decision to be baptized again. Tim's realization of his disconnection from the Catholic Church helped him move forward in his Christian faith after attending Northeast and understanding the values Jesus taught. This is the actual interview Tim and Angie gave by video to the congregation at Northeast Christian Church in 2005.

Tim: "Prior to coming to Northeast, I lacked the understanding of my baptism because I was an infant and didn't have much say about it.

Angie: "I, too, was baptized as a baby and never thought about it in depth until getting baptized at Northeast.

Tim: "My first reaction when I heard about baptism and understood what Northeast beliefs were, in my opinion I had already been baptized. Why do I need to go through it again?

Angie: "Baptism was good enough for my religion when I was an infant. Shouldn't it be good enough now? I struggled with that a lot.

Tim: "I grew up hearing readings from the Bible every Sunday morning but was never a reader of the Bible. After coming to Northeast and learning what the Bible says, I concur and accept as true that immersion is what God intended it to be.

Angie: "I had many family issues to deal with. My family is especially strong in their Catholic faith and was not comfortable with me going outside of our faith.

Tim: "I was ready to be baptized after the first six to eight weeks of coming to Northeast. Being a father, however, this is something I wanted to experience as a family.

Angie: "When I decided that I was going to be baptized, it was, honestly, because my daughter wanted to be baptized. I was having issues and struggling with the decision if I wanted to get baptized or not. My own daughter Terra came to Tim and me and said she would like to be re-baptized by immersion. I decided immediately that this is right. This is the right time. Terra was going up on stage to the baptismal and [would] be baptized, and then she [would] baptize me. That is how we accomplished it. Actually, for me, it was not something I had planned for weeks in advance. Having made a quick decision, after months of struggling, I decided to be baptized and have my daughter do it.

Tim: "My baptism was really cool. My brother and I were on a family vacation last October in Florida. We were at the beach in the Gulf of Mexico, and I turned to my brother and said, "Nick, I am ready to be baptized, and I would like for you to do it for me right now."

Nick is Tim's younger brother. He is a former Catholic who had been baptized by immersion in a Protestant church earlier.

Tim: "We proceeded and I was fully immersed right there in the Gulf of Mexico. I came up out of the water really feeling like a different person. I was thinking, what a way to be baptized in front of God and his vast nature.

Angie: "Once I decided that I was going to be baptized, I didn't think about it; however, once it was over, I had a whole new cleansing feeling of renewed life. I cannot describe in words the feeling it gave me internally. A closeness to God that I had not experienced in a long, long time.

" I wish my parents would accept that what I am doing is bringing me closer to God instead of the thought, 'I am going outside their religion.' And not that I am practicing the faith, but I am doing what is right for me. It has been incredibly difficult. That is what made this whole thing hard. God was not my struggle. It was my struggle with my family about God."[5]

You will find countless stories similar to Tim and Angie's struggle to depart from traditional practices.

Another example is Debbie, a clinical nurse specialist and educator. She travels all over the country teaching at conferences for hospitals and nursing organizations, speaking to hundreds of people weekly. Debbie Tuggle was outgoing and spoke her mind. Debbie grew up Catholic and shared—by email—some of her personal thoughts with me regarding baptism. The following is the an email I received in 2002:

Sent: Wednesday, August 07, 2002 3:45 p.m.
To:Timlott@necchurch.org
Subject: From Deb

Dear Tim,

I attended the Discovery class last night. I cried in my car on the way home and again when I woke up at 3:00 a.m. The reason for me being upset surrounds the "correct" way to be baptized by immersion. I tried to understand this and asked the instructor to make me feel better about it. He tried, but I was not comforted. Saying I have to repeat it all over again and do it correctly Biblically made me unhappy. The first time was not right, so I needed to do it again is how I feel. I know that I was only an infant, but I have recommitted to the Lord through confirmation and countless other personal gestures of faith. To me, it is like being married for twenty-five years, and having someone tell me that the sacrament of marriage we entered into was not real or good enough, and that we had to repeat it again, starting all over. In agreeing to be re-baptized, I feel like I would be saying my children and all my Catholic relatives are pagans or inferior in their faith.

In some way, this does not feel right, especially the part whereby any person that has been baptized by immersion is able to baptize me. My husband was immersed and he is an extremely casual Christian and only a occasional attendee. I am far more involved in my faith than he will ever be and I was only "sprinkled," as it was referred to. By the way, I do not like my baptism referred to as a "sprinkling." My baptism means a lot more to me than that, and it feels like an insult to make light of it.

I know Jesus Christ. I have a personal relationship with Him, a deep one. I tithe and then some. I participate in ministry; however, I don't feel God moving me to do this. I will pray on it and will listen hard to His answer. As of this moment, I do not see it happening. Maybe after the "Catholic" class I will feel differently. I don't know. I guess what I am saying is if I must be an official member to continue as Medical Ministry Coach, you may need to start recruiting for a replacement. I hope that will not be the case.

Thanks, Tim, sorry to dump this on you before the Summit. We will talk at some point.

[Two years later.]

Sent: Friday, September 23, 2005 1:46 p.m.
To: Bob Cherry
Subject: Be blessed! Debbie

Hi Bob,
    I wanted to touch base with you before Sunday. Even though I

speak publicly to hundreds of people multiple times per month, I am simply unable to talk about my faith without choking up. This is extremely emotional for me. I simply could not explain to you last weekend why I have made the decision at this time. Well, here it is! Last Sunday, you finally gave a sermon addressing baptism that did not offend my Catholic heritage or my rebellious nature one bit. Maybe I have become accustomed to the subject. Maybe I have lost my stubbornness. Either way, your analogy regarding the tornado coming really worked for me. As you said, a person would do anything in their power to save their life in that situation, and I decided my eternal life is far more important than my earthly one.

I do not profess to believe that immersion is the only way. I know God loves me and I have had a personal relationship with Jesus for as far back as I can remember. I do not necessarily hear Him telling me I need to do this; I simply want to do it in case it might please Him. I was actually upset with God after Katrina. What man does to man—Sept. 11 for example—I can chalk up to free will; however, when nature hits so hard, I have trouble understanding. I was in a funk for several days and in small ways like the attached message, he has shown me His love and presence in little miracles, I will not go into detail here.

By the way, Tim Lott called. Thanks for telling him. I so wish that I could have reached this point before he left. He worked so hard with me. Tim said he was going to share my story with his "Growing up Catholic" class in Florida. If you want to comment on the fact that I was raised Catholic in hopes of encouraging other Catholics to consider immersion, I am fine with that. I am assuming you will be the one baptizing me, right? I certainly thought it would be Tim, but I would really be honored if you could.
-Debbie

I received the following email two days later from Debbie.

Sent: Sunday, September 25, 2005 8:28 p.m.
To: Tim Lott
Subject: Debbie

This was the big day. Bob did a great job in your absence. I was a wreck; luckily, Bart was opening up the service and spaced, forgetting that there was a baptism. Bob and I merely stood there in the pool until someone reminded him, but it was funny and broke the tension. I was thankful for that because I was on the verge of tears and did not want to blubber in front of the entire congregation. I had planned to answer the question, "Is Jesus your personal Lord and savior?" with "He always has been and always will be," but I could only get out "indeed," which I tried to say with enthusiasm. After it was over, I thought that I would collapse and did so in the changing room. I was so overwhelmed with happiness. I think Bob wondered why I was so slow in there. Hilary met me when I came out, we prayed together and it was so great. Thank you, thank you for all of your support. Hope you get up this way again sometime. Say hello to Genora.[6]

-Debbie

From my personal experiences and speaking to others contemplating being re-baptized, I found that fear of how the family will respond and personal pride of the deep rooted Catholicism is the biggest roadblock standing in the way of a person accepting Jesus fully, dying to his or her old self and making Him the Lord and Savior through re-baptism.

Every situation will be different, and when it comes to family, using common sense and finding personal quality time to share your heart will benefit everyone. This one act could possibly crumble the brick wall that has been built up for so long, bringing you and your family closer together. Let them see your changed heart by your actions from what you are now experiencing for the first time in your life. You will make a huge impact on them.

STUDY GUIDE QUESTIONS

CHAPTER ELEVEN

I Have A Decision To Make

SMALL GROUP OR CLASS LEADER: Review chapter ten. As the group is entering the room, ask each individual to think about and answer this question: In what areas of your life are you willing to attempt the impossible? Have them write their answers in the book. Give a few minutes for everyone to participate. Ask several people to share what they wrote.

1.

2.

3.

4.

Q: What are the five top priorities in your life?
1.

2.

3.

4.

5.

Q: Take this quiz. Does any of the following describe you?_____
You are in control of your life.
You are in harmony with everyone.
You have no uncertainties.
You need no pardons from anyone.

Q: Describe someone you know who fits one of those statements.

Q: From the above quiz which of the four causes you the most struggle? Explain.

Q: Why is it that the one who most needs a relationship with Jesus resists Him so much. Why do you think this is true?

Q: Would you say that you are in a self-protective or humbling frame of mind when it comes to making a decision to accept Christ as your Lord and Savior by being re-baptized? Describe your thoughts and why.

Q: What does the term "born again" mean to you. Explain

Q: When should someone be baptized?

Q: Does a person's age make a difference?

Q: Do you believe infants or young children understand the commitment of accepting Christ and being baptized? Whether yes or no, explain your answer.

Was the ritual of baptizing infants established by man-made beliefs? Circle: Yes or No.

LEADER: Read the following aloud, ask those who have a Bible to turn to the verses given below. After reading, discuss what it means to be capable of accepting Jesus as your Lord and Savior.

The practice of baptizing infants came around 400 A.D. A man named Augustine came up with the idea of "original sin." This basically meant that everyone inherits the sin of Adam at birth and is therefore separated from God from the beginning of their lives. Of course, that caused parents to become concerned over the fate of their children, should they die before "getting right with God." Because it is risky to immerse an infant, those people decided to sprinkle them with water instead. Consequently, both baptizing infants and baptizing by sprinkling came from human ideas. They are not found in the Bible.

If we look in the Bible, we see that children are never seen to "accept Christ"—and therefore get right with God. But interestingly enough, God never tells us what to do to keep a child safe. Did He forget that important point, letting many children go to Hell and suffer eternally? No. A child is safe in the arms of God until he or she is capable of understanding how to be saved by accepting Jesus as a personal Savior (See 2 Samuel chapter 12, verses 22 and 23 along with Matthew chapter 18 verse 10). Thus, only adults and older children—those who can understand separation from God because of sin—are at the age when acceptance of Christ is possible.[11]

THINK ON THIS: "He who has the Son has life; he who does not have the Son of God does not have life" (1 John 5:12).

Jesus is the chosen one. He offers us life if we choose to follow Him. The major part of living a better life is surrendering our way of dictating our own life and following His way of living. Knowing this, would you consider starting a new adventure, with Christ? _____.

What Do I Say To My Family?

"I feel that I have failed as a mother."
                                    - Judy Lott, November 1998

It can be said with some certainty that our families are taken
into consideration when we are faced with making an important decision. If you were notified of the opportunity to transfer
out of state, you would naturally consult with your family first.
When planning a summer vacation, you confer with your immediate
family on where they would like to go. If you plan to purchase a new
or used car, you would check with your spouse. If you needed an
important medical procedure, you would inform your family. When
it comes to making a decision to look at another church or being
re-baptized at another church, consulting the family can be a complicated and highly sensitive procedure.

Why do we struggle so much with family? For me and probably for you, too, it was the distinct possibility of disappointing and
embarrassing them. My whole family was Catholic. Our legacy as a
Catholic described who I was and was similar to saying, "I am an
American." Therefore, the possibility of hurting or disappointing my
family was incredibly high. I could have elected not to share anything
about my new church or what I was about to do but I did not want
them to find out from someone else as if I was hiding what I believed.
My new-found excitement in Christ was something I desperately
wanted to share with them. At the same time, I understood they
might not be willing to listen. How would I explain what it meant to
me personally to accept Jesus by my own decision and actions?

For the majority of us, being in a Catholic family meant we

went to a Catholic grade school, participated in the annual summer church picnics and played sports in the Catholic league schools. We Catholics grew up in a culture that was tightly woven. Some years later, as adults, we sometimes find ourselves looking to break away from that culture and its inheritances. The people we love and care about wonder why, suspecting that something is drastically wrong with us. The following is a true account of the conversation with my mother regarding my decision to be re-baptized by immersion in a Protestant church.

"Mom, as you know I have been attending Northeast Christian Church for some time and it has been a good experience for me. Over this period of time, I have made a decision to go deeper within myself and ask hard questions about the direction I am going as a Christian. I have connected with what is being taught at Northeast on Sundays, something that did not happen in the Catholic Church. I am here today because I want to share with you a decision I have made about my future. I quickly added, in a calm voice, my decision is about being re-baptized. Her facial expression abruptly changed to an unadorned blank stare.

I paused briefly, unsure of the reaction I would get, allowing my words to settle; then I continued. "Mom, before you say anything or make a comment, I would like for you to hear me out. When I was an infant, you and Dad made a decision for me to be baptized because I could not answer the call to live the commitment of baptism. Both you and Dad raised me responsibly as you knew best in the Catholic Church tradition. You both have done a great job. As you know, I fell out of touch with the Church because I was not relating to the mass but simply going through the motions on Sunday mornings. That is not practicing the Catholic faith we were taught or what the church expects from us." My mother leaned forward in her chair. Her facial expression was still the same blank stare and with both of her elbows on the table, she slowly placed her hands to her head and looked down in silence.

As she listened intently I continued "I was being a hypocrite. I called myself a Catholic, but I was not following or practicing what the church expected of a true Catholic."

"Mom, there has been a void deep within me for a long time. It is difficult to explain exactly what that emptiness is but I can tell you it's as if something has been missing. I know now what needs to be done and I'm asking you to understand what I am about to say."

"What do you mean?" she asked.

I looked across the table at her and said, "On Sunday, December 21st, I am going to be re-baptized by immersion."

I paused for a moment, waiting for an outburst, she said nothing. I continued because she did not show any reaction. "I needed to make this decision from my heart to accept Jesus myself. I am not a freak joining a cult or anything like that. I have not gone off the deep end either. I am the same person you've known for thirty-eight years, but I've changed on the inside".

It was so quiet you could hear the second hand tick on the wall clock. I sat in silence waiting for a reply, listening to the second hand tick off the seconds. She broke the silence and said, "I feel as if I have failed as a mother."

"What!" I said. "Failed as a mother? What are you saying?" I looked down at the floor and shook my head in disbelief. "Do you really think you have failed, Mom? Deep inside do you really feel that you have totally failed as a mother? You know who I have become and what I am about; I have overcome battles I never thought I could overcome, accomplished much more than I expected. You and Dad instilled your traits in me, which assisted in making it possible for me to overcome all of those obstacles that I faced. As we sit here, are you able to look at me in the eyes and truthfully say that you have failed as a mother?"

With a sigh and a dejected voice she said, "Well, I feel as if I have failed in some aspects of the Catholic Church."

"Because I want to be baptized again does not mean you or Dad have failed at anything," I said. "Let me explain it this way. Doing this means, I will be making my own decision to show Jesus I want to follow Him. Thirty-eight years ago you and Dad made a decision for me; now I need to make the decision for myself." As Mom sat back in the white, high-back kitchen chair, I saw the tension that was once etched on her face start to fade away.

I continued to explain. "We can both agree the reason for my baptism as an infant was so I would eventually see Christ one day in heaven. That is exactly the same thing I want, precisely as you and Dad had hoped. This is why I personally need to show Him by making my own decision with my own heart, being re-baptized by immersion exactly as Jesus Himself. "Mom, there is too much at stake for me not to go through with this."

She replied, "I am actually happy for you, however, I am hurt not because of your newfound happiness in another church, but your condemnation of my church."

I inhaled deeply and slowly explained, "I am not making a judgmental announcement that the Catholic Church does not do a lot of good for people—quite the contrary. The Church has many organizations that help thousands of distressed people such as the Catholic Charities; the relief efforts the Catholic Church is involved in all over the world are astounding. However, I have disagreements on certain practices and beliefs the Church teaches Mom. Because I have those disagreements does not mean I intentionally want to hurt you, Dad or the Catholic Church. I would prefer you both celebrate with me in the same way as when you baptized me as an infant.

"Come to the nine-fifteen service at Northeast with me in two weeks." I was not sure of the type of response I would get, knowing they had never attended a Protestant service. This would be really stepping out of their comfort zone. So I said, "I understand if you do not want to attend the service, and I value your reasons why. You do not have to answer at this time; you and Dad think it over."

I am disclosing this conversation because it may be a useful tool in approaching your own family. I found that being honest and sharing my heart was a comforting factor for me when I spoke to both of them about this taboo subject. Both my mother and father received my decision fairly well. Unfortunately, some people never reach this point with their families, but I implore you not to wait until they are on their deathbed to explain your belief and why. You will forever regret it.

By finding another church and taking the step to bury my old nature and becoming a new person through my full acceptance of Christ by being re-baptized, I found how important that one act was and how it affected my inner being, although it was complicated to express in words to those I loved.

You, too, will experience this new understanding of church is not only moving, but also exciting and life-changing, which can be exceptionally complex to explain. Be conscious of the fact that those you love may not want to hear about it. You may find yourself wondering if you will be accepted in the family after trying to explain. Will my husband or wife go to church with me, or not go at all? Could telling my spouse how I feel cause strife between us? In addition, what about our children and the sound foundation I want them to grow up with? These may become your concerns; those people who have attended the "Growing up Catholic" classes have expressed the same fears. You are not alone in your apprehensions. I was disturbed that my mother would continue to judge herself as a mother who failed.

I honestly looked at my situation like this—family or Jesus? If my family had disagreed with my decision or would not have supported me, there is no doubt I would have chosen Christ and gone through with my re-baptism. Reading in scripture what He instructed us to do was something I could not overlook.

Debbie DeMont's personal story: Debbie DeMont is a professional photographer who has studios in Los Angeles, California, and Fort Lauderdale, Florida. She grew up Catholic in California where she met her husband John at the age of thirty-six. Before meeting John, she explained, "After leaving home I have been searching for different churches that would work for me," Debbie said. "I knew John was different when we met. He would talk about his family and ask a lot of questions about me. It was obvious John's focus was not on himself. Most everyone I knew or dated boasted about how much they owned and what they had achieved. It is so clear to me now why John is the person he is, but in actuality, I did not understand completely why until later in our marriage."

"My process of realizing Jesus was my Lord and Savior did not happen quickly. John never pushed his beliefs on me; he did not need to because I observed and saw for myself through our marriage. I never knew what unconditional love was until I met my husband, who at the time was attending a Protestant church. It was then that I discovered God has unconditional love for me too."

"What helped make my breakthrough a long process is when I was young; my parents drove us kids to mass every Sunday morning. They did not actually go to church with us, but we all were taught the foundational beliefs and went through the process of confirmation and then making our first communion, as everyone else did. At the time, I did not understand what the sacrament meant, but I do remember being excited about wearing my new white dress and new white shoes as my relatives took pictures of everyone standing in line to receive communion from the priest."

"From a very young age, though, I knew my Catholic background ran deep, so deep, in fact, my first instinct was to call and ask permission from my parents about being re-baptized. I was fifty years old. I decided to not ask permission; after all, I am a grown adult who knew the importance of the decision I was making. When I did share the news with my parents, I showed them the actual baptism on video tape. Unfortunately, the reception I received was less than enthusiastic. They acted bored and believed I was on another adventure. This saddens me more than being hurt that they were not interested in my baptism. I do not believe they know God. I hope somehow they will hear, see, or maybe read this book so it will help them to understand. I want to reach out to them so badly."[1]

A time may come when you will need to look at what is more important, perhaps as Debbie has done. Jesus has told us that no one comes before Him. Your relationship with Jesus is far more important than struggling with the emotional drain of family, if it reaches that point. But the good news is they are able to witness the change within you by simply observing your actions and words. This does not mean being "odd for God" and driving everyone away from you by constantly bringing up religious beliefs and reciting Bible verses.

I have known a few people who would not say anything to their families because of the uproar it would cause. When the holidays came around or anytime during family gatherings, the unspoken rule about the subject of religion is that it is outlawed. Family and relatives acted indifferently toward each other because of someone's new faith. They would shove the most important blessing from God under the rug, forgetting about it until a crisis struck. Subsequently, during the crisis, members of the family were at odds with each other.

I have also known married couples who have divorced because one spouse went to a Catholic church and the other to a Protestant church. This has a tendency to happen when one person is overbearing and forces his or her faith onto the spouse in a negative way. They push the differences of their church's beliefs and its teachings in each other's face. This is hurtful to anyone, but especially a spouse. Eventually, the battle turns to the kids. What church should they attend? What type of kids' programming and teachings will that church have? In the end, there is so much anger built up that the family is ripped apart, accomplishing exactly the opposite of what God wants.

The best example I can give on how to approach a spouse is my own wife. She handled our situation the way I think most married couples should handle the sensitive subject of going to a Protestant church rather than a Catholic church.

Throughout the whole time we dated and later after we were married, Genora never pressured me to attend a Protestant church service or change my faith. She neither attacked my faith nor degraded the traditions or rituals that made up a big part of my Catholic belief.

By merely setting an example in different ways, Genora attracted my attention. I noticed she would read a brief section in the Bible before going to bed every night. She would read a book called *My Utmost for His Highest*, by Oswald Chambers, published by Discovery House in 1992. I began to realize those were her daily devotions, comforting and aiding her with the stresses of work and everyday life. Occasionally, she would go over the notes from service on Sunday. Genora never positioned herself or her faith above me, as though to say I am better than you.

Because of her ethical approach, I became conscious this was not a demonstration or a performance she was putting on to teach or pressure me.

Micki Jerry's personal story: Being logical, along with setting the example yourself, could be the first step in getting your spouse or family to understand why you are so adamant about your new life change.

Micki Jerry is a busy wife and mom. She and her husband, Kevin, have an eight-year-old son, Brock. Micki grew up Catholic. Her father was on the Board of Directors at Saint Meinrad Seminary for twenty-five years. Her mother serves communion to shut-ins. Micki's uncle was a Maryknoll missionary –a Catholic order of missionaries— in Japan and was Secretary to the Vatican. Micki has been re-baptized. I want to share her story with you, as she told it to the "Growing up Catholic" class at Northeast.

"My brothers and sisters would email me spiritual prayers of support, but they were afraid to talk about God in person. Our family never read the Bible growing up, and it's probably safe to say that not one of my siblings owns a Bible or reads one. I recently asked my mom why we were never exposed to the Bible. Her answer was, and I quote, 'We did not have to read it, we lived it.' I looked her in the eye and asked, 'What does that mean?' She had no answer."

"Several weeks later I gave her a copy of a *Quest Study Bible* and showed her how easy it was to find topics and how easy it was to read, etc. She thanked us and several weeks later returned the Bible, thanking me for loaning it to her. I told her that I wanted her to keep it, and she said, 'That's okay.'"

"I left the Catholic Church to attend Northeast in January of 2002. I was fulfilling a New Year's resolution more than actually looking for God. I had told my husband that because our son was born in 1998, we needed to go to church as a family. I thank Bob Cherry for being at the beginning of a sermon series on financial peace the first time we attended; it brought us back. Within several weeks, we attended a Discovering Northeast class, after pretty much deciding we had found home. I remember crying as I watched the videos of awestruck Christians being baptized on the large side screens in church, leaning over to Kevin saying, 'I have already been baptized,' yet wondered why I was crying."

"Bob was there for the beginning of the class; he went over the Nine Values of Northeast Christian church. I remember him talking about unchurched people and how it was up to us to bring them to Christ. I was tremendously sad, though, already feeling a calling to be of some assistance to my Catholic friends and family members by receiving Christ in the same way I had been learning to receive Him. Bob has probably read those Nine Values to countless thousands over the last twenty some years. I am sure he can perform his talk sleepwalking. For me, it was the first time in my life that anyone held me accountable for my own soul."

"After living my relatively unexciting life as a Catholic—except that I was an unbelievable sinner—I found myself in love with an amazing man who had been divorced. He agreed to seek an annulment so we could be married in a Catholic Church. We started the process, and about three weeks later I was receiving phone calls from several members of Kevin's family, stating that they were 'uncomfortable' with the level of questioning from the Catholic Priests calling them—in New Jersey—regarding Kevin's past. I put a halt to it immediately and sought to be married by a Christian minister."

"When I called the priest to explain we preferred not to continue the process, he advised me that as a Catholic, if I went through with marriage to this man, I could no longer receive communion in the Catholic Church. I called another priest and got the same answer. After the third priest said the same thing, I said, 'What if I take it anyway?' He said, 'It wouldn't mean anything.' I was upset, but unsettled. I failed to consider for a minute that Jesus Christ did not want to be in my life. After Kevin and I were married, I continued to go to the Catholic Church for eight years. We baptized our son Catholic. Kevin would attend Catholic mass with me once a year, maybe, and fell well short of getting anything out of the mass."

"My decision to be re-baptized was not an easy one at first. I was sure God saw me as a baptized believer. I told my husband, as he was insisting we needed to be re-baptized, that I needed to study and prepare for the decision I was about to make. Not wanting to approach this lightly, I wanted to be ready. Truthfully, I was buying time, because I was not buying into the fact that I legitimately needed to be re-baptized. For me to walk into that baptismal font and not deem it was necessary would make me the biggest hypocrite of all time."

"As I continued my reading of the Bible and studying with other Christians, not one thing convinced me; it was many things. I was beginning to see I was becoming 'new.' I was no longer living a secular life, but was actually waking up every morning asking God what I could do for him this day, no longer praying to Him and asking for help with what I had going on. I started completely trusting that I would be taken care of, and I decided not to bargain for the gifts He would bestow on me. Baptism became, for me, not something I had to do for my Church, but something I wanted to do for God. For me, it was a way of moving my relationship with God to the next level. I could not wait to follow in Jesus' footsteps as He walked into the Jordan River with John the Baptist, setting the ultimate example for the rest of us. God knew what was in my heart. I was starting my life over, and what better way to symbolize the change in me?"

"Those of you in this class, if for whatever reason, are not feeling compelled to be baptized, I would back off and suggest more self-searching. I don't think that it's important to commit right now, because you may be feeling pressured, but commit to working through the possibility of being baptized. If you are truly working to uncover the mystery of what God has planned for you and seeking answers through scripture, other Christians, and prayer, the truth about baptism will be revealed to you."[2]

Over time, Micki and Kevin found a true, meaningful relationship with Christ, but not before encountering disagreements from family and the church itself. The authenticity regarding re-baptism was revealed to me as well; however, I will never forget Mom's words: "I feel as if I have failed as a mother." Misunderstandings and disagreements can and will occur between your spouse, family members or friends around the subject of re-baptism by immersion. Conflict is so tempting. But a better solution is to address your concerns directly in a gentle and honest manner. You also need to carefully choose the appropriate time to discuss your feelings calmly.

Here are a few suggestions that may help. Write down what you need to say and bring your notes with you. For those who have harsh parents or family members who may not be willing to listen, sit down and write a letter, explaining in a loving way why you are attending a Protestant church. Explain the reason you are choosing this particular time in your life to be re-baptized. Write down exactly what your heart is telling you. Your parents must know and understand they did not fail raising you Catholic.

The Catholic Church is all your parents knew. That is what their parents knew and how they grew up. Undoubtedly, they will see the true intentions in your heart by reading your letter. Give them the opportunity to read your words and identify the reasons why you are making this choice. Reading the letter provides them time to think and reflect instead of jumping and reacting without fully hearing you out; giving them this opportunity could result in a positive outcome for everyone.

December 21, 1998, the day had arrived. Two weeks after inviting my parents, I was going to be baptized. The photo is forever etched in my mind of me sitting with my parents at the 9:15 a.m. service. This was the first time they had been to Northeast since our wedding in the small chapel nine years earlier, now they were walking into an auditorium that seated one thousand people. They quickly noticed how things had changed over the years. As we walked to our seats, I explained that I needed to go backstage for a few minutes toward the end of service and I would meet them shortly afterward in the lobby.

During service, when it came time for me to leave, I made my way behind the stage. Still wondering what Mom and Dad were thinking as they sat at the service, nervously I slipped into my swimming trunks and put the white gown that was provided over my head. *This is it.* As I walked to the baptismal pool behind the curtain, I was thinking, *what a long road to get to this point.* Bob, who had finished his sermon, rushed to meet me while the worship team sang and played music. Bob and I walked down into the water which came chest high; then the massive curtain opened, exposing both of us in the baptistery. The lights were bright, but I could tell the auditorium was completely full. Bob introduced me and said a few words, then asked, "Tim is Jesus your Lord and Savior?"

Instantly my mind flashed back to the day I was in Bob's office on my knees asking Christ to come into my life.

"Yes," I said firmly. With that, I was underwater. As I came up out of the water, I heard the roar of thunderous clapping in celebration and joy for me. Glancing at my mother and father, to my surprise, they too were both applauding. That was a big moment for me. Before leaving the baptismal on stage, I noticed Genora was standing against the back wall directly in front of us; she too was clapping with a big smile on her face. I was not aware she would be attending the service that morning, but what an enormous and pleasant surprise it was to see her there.

CHAPTER TWELVE

What Do I Say To My Family?

SMALL GROUP OR CLASS LEADER: Review chapter eleven. Take ten minutes and ask the group to share their own story as it pertains to attending the Protestant church and how it may have affected their family members?

Ask the following questions:

Do you have room for dialogue when speaking to your family or a spouse, or is the subject closed? What do you fear when it comes to sharing with loved ones what you have discovered at another church?

Why do you believe they do not understand your new enthusiasm for church? What made you decide to accept Christ into your heart as your Lord and Savior?

Q: As an individual or group, answer the following questions:

If you are attending another church, does your family know? If yes, what was their reaction? How did it make you feel?

Q: Have you been re-baptized? If so, have you told your family? If not, why? If yes, did they support you?

Q: What was their reaction?

Q: If you are currently attending a Protestant church or have been re-baptized by immersion, what change or changes are evident in you that your family can see? Describe those changes below.

When speaking to loved ones about changing your faith or being re-baptized, a great deal of care must be taken. Parents or spouses do not need to feel threatened or abandoned. Speak humbly to prevent tensions from building to the point of an argument, which possibly could divide the family. You want to communicate in a redemptive manner. I suggest starting out this way: "I want to thank you for raising me in a Christian tradition. You are going to be so glad to know that I have made a commitment to Christ, making Him my personal Lord and Savior. I want to build upon what you have started so long ago when you baptized me as an infant. I feel as if it is an adventure and not a duty."

LEADER: Give the group a few minutes to think about what they would say to their own family. The following can be used as a class discussion. Think about how you will approach your family. Take a moment and write out a few sentences of what you might say to them. Let your heart speak. Use the above suggestion, if needed, to get you started.

If you have a good deal of resistance after bringing up the subject and anticipate resentment, here is a helpful solution. Explain the reasons you are choosing this particular time in your life to be re-baptized. List those reasons below.

HELPFUL WRITING TIP: Now take the reasons from above and put them in a letter to your parents. This tool could also be used for a spouse. You may choose to read the letter aloud rather than giving it them in an envelope if appropriate.

It is important to remember that your parents did what was right in their eyes because of their love for you. This can be a wonderful opportunity to reach out to your parents or spouse. If you have had past differences, it is now time to deposit those feelings in the incinerator and move on by sharing the change in you with your family.

Explain that there are thousands of people who have been baptized with water but show no evidence of change. Those people still love the sin they practice; they have no fear of God, nor do they respect His commandments. They are in charge of their own lives. You want to change how you live life. You want to turn your control of how you live over to God.

Review the questions and your answers in this chapter. Have you learned something that is especially helpful? If so, write it here and explain how it can help you.

THINK ON THIS: Baptism is not an outward cleaning, but saves us through an inward cleaning. It is an appeal to God for a good conscience and asks God to take away the guilt of our past sin that Christ paid for, wiping our 'inner slate' clean. 1 Peter 3: 21 "and this water symbolizes baptism that now saves you also—not the removal of dirt from the body but the pledge of a good conscience toward God. It saves you by the resurrection of Jesus Christ."

The Unimaginable Occurs

Seven months had passed since my re-baptism. Genora continued to live at her friend Debbie's house during that time. As a replacement for working long hours, I started to come home on time and volunteer at church. I was handy with a hammer, so without asking, I added new cabinets and wire shelving and installed a side-by-side industrial refrigerator in the incredibly small staff kitchen, which doubled for preparing communion on the weekends.

Volunteers were needed for various tasks around the church campus, such as cleaning the baptistery and preparing communion for each weekend service. I jumped right in and started helping where I could. That achieved two things for me—it kept me from coming home to an empty house late at night, and I found myself wanting to help where I was needed but trying to keep a low profile.

With all of the problems I had gone through over the year, my life had changed drastically, to say the least. The goal of making a lot of money and proving to myself that I could be a major player with all of the luxuries that came with the title was no longer important. My adventure with Christ, growing closer to Him on an everyday basis and accepting the reality of letting Him, not me, run my life was getting easier. God changes us from the inside out so I applied those changes I learned to my own life. During this time, I also discovered what Genora meant by "growing." When I look back now the best way I can describe it is I had become a robot -for lack of a better term- on Sunday mornings. The Catholic Church did not encourage me to grow in the same manner Genora meant by growing. From my youth to an adult, I had been pre-programmed to follow the churches teachings only to become disconnected by the rituals I practiced, instead of learning to grow closer to God.

As the months passed, Genora and I both witnessed changes in each other, especially in me. We started to date again in October of 1999, deciding it was best not to jump right back into a full-fledged relationship. We started seeing Cheri, a Christian counselor on staff at church. Unknown to me, during those seven months, Genora had been getting reports that my agenda and priorities had changed.

Genora and Tim Lott

Cheri assisted us in communicating in a healthier way. Truthfully, before I welcomed Jesus into my heart and before I let God start running my life, I would probably not have seen a counselor. No doubt, my self-pride would have stood in the way. "A counselor? We don't need a counselor. We can work this out on our own." Let's face it, we men can be hardheaded at times.

As a side note: Men, if you are at a point in your life where you need to seek counseling, listen to me. A real man shows his intelligence by seeking advice and guidance, including support from other trusted men and a Christian counselor. You are the leader of your household; set the example as a leader and do what does not come naturally. Get help for your own good and that of your family.

I continued to volunteer in different ministries at church and became friends with those I served with on a regular basis. Life was moving on and so were the counseling sessions. Dating went extremely well for both Genora and me, and Genora moved back home. We started our lives together all over again after nine years. Living a Christian marriage as a couple was wonderful.

One night after dinner, I received a phone call from Bob Cherry. He asked me to attend a leadership conference with some of the church staff and a few other volunteers. He said, "We will be in Chicago for four days. Can you get off from work?"

I managed to take a couple days off and joined them; however, I didn't expect to see more than seven thousand people in attendance at a leadership conference. The speakers were high-profile, successful executives from different organizations and companies all over the United States. They shared their leadership techniques and knowledge, as everyone listened intently.

Strangely, what was said from the stage, as I sat in the second day's session of the conference, literally hit me full force. I had to hold back from physically jumping out of my seat. I brought attention to myself by suddenly jerking forward and clinching my fists pumping them vigorously in the air in rapid succession, but only softly whispering, "Yes, yes, that's it!" Those around me gave a few odd stares, but the host of the conference said, "The hope of the world is through the local church." I realized at that moment why the Protestant church made such an impact on me. The reason I connected with the Protestant church so easily was that its members devoted themselves to the apostles' teaching and fellowship, to the breaking of bread and to prayer. They praised God and enjoyed the favor of all the people, exactly as it says in Acts 2. In other words, their doors were open to everyone, not judging or condemning me for my past. Acts 2:47 says, "And the Lord added to their number daily those who were being saved." I had experienced a life change after hitting rock bottom. Until that time, I did not want, or believe I needed a change. In fact, I was one of the saved because of an open door.

Sitting there in that huge auditorium, I realized people are merely changed by the lessons learned and by the power of God. All I needed was to let God into my life, and when that happened, He filled the emptiness within me.

Sitting there my thoughts immediately went directly to all of those people who were simply going through the mechanics of church and living life their way, hearts coated with a protective sealant so nothing penetrates, in order to hide the emptiness they are experiencing. The Protestant church opened its door for me as it has for so many others because no one cared if I was Catholic, Presbyterian, Methodist, Mormon, Muslim, or any other faith. The leaders only encouraged me to open my heart and see what Christ had to say through the Bible. Until I was willing to accept church in a different setting, I was unwilling to change or be open to identify with God's word. I finally accepted and understood that getting close to God was not about going to mass and feeling comfortable that I had received communion, or praying to Mary, asking her to carry my prayers to Jesus. Having a relationship with God was about getting to know Him on an authentic and personal level.

I continued volunteering and lending a hand when needed around the church, including building teams of volunteers for various ministry tasks. In March of 2000 the position of Director of Ministries came open. Rob Kastens, Executive Director at Northeast, came to me and asked, "Would you like to interview for the job?"

My first response was, "Are you kidding? I'm not worthy to be on a church staff." My second response had been more direct, "Do you realize who you're asking? I have been separated from my wife, grew up Catholic, I don't have a Protestant background and never attended a Bible college or had previous experience working in a church. I've never taught, and my speaking ability is not perfect. Why in the world would you want someone like me to interview for this position?"

Rob interrupted me saying, "I have seen how you are around other volunteers and how you involved teams of people to help do the different tasks. This is the type of person we're looking for."

Hearing what Rob said gave me some comfort and confidence, but in reality, what I was doing was using common sense.

After talking to my wife and praying about the interview, my thought was, *if God had a plan for me, I should not stand in the way.* Remembering how I used to run my own life, I did not want to get back in that mode again. At the time, I worked as a supervisor. *If this is meant to happen, it will,* I thought.

The interview was on a Tuesday afternoon in late March. A week later, Rob called to welcome me to the church staff as the new Director of Ministries. How ironic that he called April 1, April Fools Day. After the shock of hearing the news, I thought, *God sure does have a sense of humor,* as I nervously wondered what He had planned for me.

Three years had passed since I was asked to come on staff building new ministries and connecting people to those ministries. In the Spring of 2003, an elder of the church approached me. He said, "Tim, we elders have watched you and feel it is time you become ordained."

I was astonished hearing this news and completely caught off guard. Stunned and lost for words I laughed aloud again, finally saying, "Do you seriously know who you are asking? What about my training? I don't think I am qualified for such a position."

He said, "Tim, your training has taken place on the job for the past three years here at Northeast." Not having a reply to his statement, I just sat there and thought to myself, *God, you know I am not worthy of this calling. Why me of all people?*

Being ordained was an extremely serious step; there were numerous questions and thoughts filled my mind. I was not sure this was something I wanted. I was somewhat apprehensive, knowing God would hold me to a higher standard of living. In my mind, I was not worthy to be an ordained minister. The thought of pursuing such a position had never crossed my mind. The question bouncing around in my head for days was, *"Who am I to become an ordained minister?"* After countless prayers and questions, I recognized that God was continuing to work His plan for me. Besides, everything that had taken place since I started my adventure with Jesus three years ago was none of my doing. How could I possibly stand in the way now?

My thoughts shifted to my parents: what would they think? And what would my friends say? Growing up Catholic and becoming an ordained Christian minister was not a common practice. Would they treat me the same or act indifferent toward me? All I wanted was to serve God and assist others as He saw fit.

Since that day on my knees in the church office, my life has been an adventure, an exhilarating roller coaster ride, with me hanging on tightly, changing sharply and significantly. Unquestionably, I was not the type to work in a church. I never once thought about being a Christian minister. Now I sometimes use that same room where I once was on my knees to help others through their difficult times. Looking back, the divorce that nearly took place between Genora and me turned out to be paramount in our lives together. We are now forever closer and stronger in our marriage bond.

The Unimaginable Occurs

GROUP OR CLASS LEADER: Review chapter twelve. As people enter the room, ask everyone to write down something that has happened in their lives that was extra-ordinary or completely unimaginable. Next, ask a few volunteers to share their experiences using the space provided below.

LEADER: Use the following questions as discussion questions:

Q. Have you ever considered that God has a plan for you? Do you know what that plan may be?

Q. What do you think God's purpose was for you by reading this book?

Q. Tim said, "I now know what Genora meant by growing." What does growing maturely in Christ mean to you? Explain your thoughts.

Q. Have you prayed, asking God to give you guidance? Take a moment to write a short prayer, asking Him to show you how to live your life.

Ask Him to give you the courage that is needed in order to change and follow His way and not your own.

THINK ON THIS: Jesus wants the best for us. He never said everything would be easy in our new-found life in Him. We sometimes learn hard lessons because He wants us to turn to Him and grow closer in our relationship.

I recommend reading the "Purpose Driven Life" by Rick Warren.

An Alternative Choice

When Raymond Moody published his famous book on near-death experiences, *Life after Life*, published by Bantam Books in 1975, it met great skepticism. Near-death experiences were thought to be outlandish, but from the hundreds of studies that have been done on the subject, they are remarkably common. Patrick Glynn, in his book *God the Evidence*, published by Three Rivers Press, describes the figure of Jesus prominently recurring in the form of a person as a "Being of Light" in near-death experiences.

Those near-death experiencers, who claim to encounter Jesus, reported being struck by an overwhelming sense of unconditional love and compassion emanating from Him. Glynn tells about George Ritchie's experience: "Ritchie described Jesus as a man made of Light, mixing primeval antiquity with vast sophistication. This person was power itself, older than time, yet more modern than anyone I had ever met."

Ritchie explains that Jesus told him the purpose of life was to love other human beings. When Ritchie thought indignantly, someone should have told me this, the response of Jesus was simple and straightforward: "I did tell you. I told you by the life I lived. I told you by the death I died."[1]

Jesus has in fact, told us the purpose of life throughout His ministry on earth as described in the Bible. Although not solely explained by Him alone, it was also explained by those he personally knew and those who were impacted by Him. Jesus showed us the way and our obligation is to follow.

Up to this point, you have traced my personal quest for truth as it relates to my (our) Catholic faith by evaluating and questioning the different areas of beliefs in order to find true answers. For the past thirteen chapters, you have witnessed the individual suspicions, battles, and tribulations that have literally transformed my life. You have seen a man changed simply by asking Jesus to come into his life. Now it is your time to respond to the feeling in your heart and take action.

God desires to be your life coach. He wants you to achieve a better way to live all phases of your life, but He wants more than one particular part of your life. We often elect to subdivide our lives by giving God one-fourth, and we will manage the other three-fourths, ultimately discovering that it doesn't work for us in that manner. I've ascertained we must surrender and change how we manage our own lives, and listen to His word. When we do our whole thought process changes. I once heard a minister say, "When we surrender to God, we gain." I am proof those words are unmistakably true. The formula for living a better life is simple, and surrendering in order to gain is part of that formula.

Section Six illustrates how you, too, can gain. First, you will discover that facing what you fear will be your greatest reward. In Chapter fourteen, you will learn a simple, yet effective method, which you can follow by committing to what matters most, surrendering your own style of life management.

CHAPTER FOURTEEN

Changing Course

Venturing out of the environment you have known for so long requires a lot of courage. My wife and I try to go on a sailing trip each year to the British Virgin Islands. We rent a boat and sail to the different islands for ten days or so. We bareboated, which meant we were the crew.

On one particular trip, after pulling up anchor in Gorda Sound, a short distance out from the Bitter End Resort in the British Virgin Islands, we steered a course for the beautiful island of Aneganda, an Island we had not visited before but had heard was exceptionally gorgeous. Getting to the island could sometimes be a challenge, because of its low profile, being only twenty-eight feet above sea level, and because it is surrounded by coral heads. Of course, the island should be approached only in good weather.

We departed around eight o'clock in the morning so the sun would be directly overhead when we arrived, which would assist us in locating the coral much easier if we needed to do so quickly. We awoke to a spectacular morning. The water was turquoise, the sky a brilliant blue, with not a cloud to be found. A nice trade wind was blowing as we departed. It was truly a beautiful day in paradise.

As all sailors know, it's prudent to continually scan the sky and be aware of any approaching weather when on the water. In the tropics, a storm is capable of building up quickly and dissipating as fast as it started. I noticed clouds building off the horizon to the East as we sailed north beyond Gorda Sound. I brought it to Genora's attention, but didn't want to alarm her; we had a high-quality, well-built forty-one foot Island Packet Cutter underneath us. If we were caught in a storm, the robust construction that went into this boat would keep us relatively safe.

Three-quarters of the way to the island, and after watching the storm assemble for some time, I told Genora, "We have a decision to make. If we turn back now, we'll miss the storm completely." Hesitating to decide will get you into trouble every time. I could make out the storm would last for twenty or thirty minutes by how fast it was traveling over the water. We elected to stay on course for Aneganda. Genora went below and got our rain gear as I reefed (lowered) the sails to a manageable position. The wind was kicking up and I wanted to maintain control of the boat when it hit.

Neither of us had sailed through a storm before; we will avoid them at all cost. When on a sailing vacation, we don't want to worry if we are coming back home or not.

As the storm came, the winds picked up and the rain came down so hard and heavy I couldn't see more than a few feet in front of our bow. Genora stayed on deck with me so in case anything unexpected happened, she could take the helm. Keeping my eye on the compass heading, I tried to keep us on course as the boat rolled and pitched badly to the port side. Holding the wheel steady was exceptionally difficult as in thunderstorms wind gusts often come out of nowhere.

Worry filled my mind because if off course too far, the coral reefs around the Island would be a problem. Knowing we were fairly close to the Island already, it was necessary we stay on its west side. Many bareboater's have run aground, destroying their boats, because of mishaps trying to get to the Island. Some of the bareboat companies do not allow their customers to make the trip for that reason and we were not planning to be one of those statistics.

A quick glance at Genora revealed a stressed face with a bewildered look as she had a death grip on the helm support bar while I did everything in my power to keep the boat on our compass heading. Ever so often, I would loudly yell as reassurance to her: "Everything will be OK." This was for her sake and mine. The rain pelted us as if small needles were hitting our faces as it blew in under the blue bimini top, our only protection from the rain. We were soaking wet and getting cold from the fierce wind and sea spray of the waves, which were breaking over the bow at this point. The water from each wave carried back thirty feet into the cockpit.

My inner self said; *I wish I were back at anchor in Gorda Sound* where we had the 1000-foot-high mountains surrounding and protecting us like a baby in a Father's arms. Trying not to let Genora know my concern she could still see the disturbed look on my face while I wiped the pounding rain from my eyes. We both fought to keep the boat upright and on course. After about thirty-five minutes of battling and hanging on for dear life, the rain let up, along with the howling wind, as we watched the sun appear again from behind the blackened clouds.

Thankfully, the storm only lasted a short while. In our minds it had lasted more than two hours. The bruises and white knuckles proved it. Keeping a close eye on the compass constantly, we had managed to not venture off course very far. With great anticipation, I picked up my binoculars to look at the horizon. Holding onto the helm support bar, as the waves had not yet calmed, a few palm trees were barely visible. Off in the distance, the buoy markers for the channel were in sight. Ah, we'd made it. The last thing I wanted was to sail completely past the island and miss it all together.

We could have elected to turn back to the safety and comfort of Gorda Sound, with no problem at all. On the other hand, going through that gruesome storm and coming out on the other side intact, was absolutely spectacular and worth every bit of the calculated risk we took. Together we fought the storm and won. Seeing a huge rainbow appear over the island with palm trees dotting the beach was exhilarating. After having that encounter with Mother Nature, both of us had

gained more confidence in our sailing skills and made the right choice by not turning back. From the helm, I looked around as we sailed in to drop anchor; it was as if we had arrived in paradise. No more apprehension was showing on Genora's face, simply an enormous smile.

This particular story about battling that storm on a sailboat was a lot like the battle of emotions and self-doubt I went through during the process of removing my Catholic beliefs, practices, pride, and all of the baggage that went with it. For years, I felt safe and secure, not wanting to get out of my comfort zone.

Unfortunately, when the storm of my life struck, I realized what I had been holding onto was not secure. My beliefs had too many holes in them. Reality set in, and I finally came to understand and accept the changes desperately needed to reach for something trustworthy and protective. Something I could totally depend on and not hesitate or doubt for an instant that it was true and would save me when needed.

The life preserver I reached for was the goodness and grace of God and His word. This did not mean the casual acquaintance of attending church when I felt like it or just attending because my wife wanted me to go. This speaks of a genuine connection with Christ, the type of relationship where you open yourself up to being exposed. Letting your guard down and getting to know Him on a very personal level. This happens by visiting with Him not only on Sunday mornings but frequently, just as you would a good friend. In this way, I began to form a bond. The moment I stepped out of my comfort zone and straightforwardly accepted Him into my heart that October day on the church floor, my adventure with Christ became a reality. Since that moment, I have felt protected and assured that He is walking beside me. It is no wonder why I have this feeling, Jesus said, "and teach them to do everything I have told you. I will be with you always, even until the end of the world" (Matthew 28:20 CEV). I have learned to turn everything over to God. Until we accept Him fully into our hearts, we will not use the struggles of life to find God. Each of us will experience pain, sorrow, stress, disappointments, and unhappiness. It is a wonderful feeling knowing that the voice of truth is with you when hardship invades your life. I don't understand why so many people will not accept this offered peace.

Rick Michelena is a pilot for Continental Airlines. He was born into a devout Catholic family. He served as an altar boy until the age of twenty. His family attended church every week. When it was necessary, as a part of his altar boy service, he even attended mass daily. Rick attended a Catholic school and completed many CCD—Catholic Christian Doctrine—classes. What follows is Rick's story of how he was filled with self-want, the need to supervise his own life believing he had an authentic relationship with Jesus until one day, flying at 33,000 feet, he discovered the truth.

Rick said, "I eventually left the coal-mining area of my hometown and pursued a career in aviation. As I worked my way up through various levels of aviation jobs and experience, I was hired by a major U.S. air-carrier when I was twenty-seven.

"During the first day of our 'new-hire' pilot orientation class, we received our freshly issued company IDs, our initial aircraft fleet assignments, and a complete aircraft manual.

"I will never forget the instructor saying, 'Gentlemen, welcome to Continental Airlines. I will be your ground school systems instructor over the next few weeks. Before you is the Seven Twenty Seven flight manual. While you are employed as a pilot for this company, you will be required to know the information contained within it. Each of you will learn how to research and address any problems that occur while performing your duty as a pilot.

"I left ground school highly motivated and looked forward to simulator training. Before long, I was flying as a line pilot. At the same time, we began to enjoy some of the things my airline career now offered. My wife and I moved out of the mobile home we were living in and, at the age of 30, we built a brand new 4,600 square foot home. We were both driving new cars and had money in the bank.

"Despite all the material gains I had now achieved, I was not happy with my life. I knew something was missing, but at the time I did not understand it was God who was missing from my life. One day, I saw a flight attendant whom I had known years before. She told me her life was now changed and she had received Jesus Christ into her life. At that time, I backed off and said, 'That's nice, I hope you're happy,' because I wanted to get away from her.

"That was only the beginning, however, of God's placing people into my life. Others soon followed and told me about Jesus Christ and how I needed Him in my life. I dismissed most of what they said because I was a Catholic and I thought I knew Jesus Christ. Yet, God was still busy planting seeds.

"As I began to think about my own relationship with God, I soon realized I was the one who had pulled away from Him. I remembered the flight attendant and many others who had challenged me about studying the Bible. One day, I thought to myself, *If I can trust my flight manual for my career, why can't I trust the Bible for my faith?* After all, as a Catholic, I never really read or studied the Bible.

"On the night of October 03, 1993, I was flying between Las Vegas and Houston. I was flying with another Christian and had listened to him talk about Jesus Christ earlier in the trip. Over the skies of El Paso, Texas, at 33,000 feet, I asked Jesus to forgive all my sins, and I have not been the same since.

"I went home and told my wife what I had experienced, and she immediately said, 'You got saved tonight.' You see, she was a backsliding Christian who had no right to marry an unbeliever. The truth is, we nearly divorced because I was lost, and I hindered her Christian walk. Incredibly, God has restored our marriage, and we've celebrated 22 years together.

"From that day on, I earnestly began to study Scripture. I even applied to the Bible the same zeal I had for airplanes. As a result, I grew in my spiritual maturity and soon began telling others about Jesus Christ and what He had done for me. Eventually God allowed me to share the gospel with many, many other Catholics. Some of the first people I told were my family and friends. I never realized what God had planned for me. My family became extremely upset that I had left the Catholic Church and were convinced I was the one in error. This led me into an even greater reliance upon the Bible.

"I soon realized God's will could never go against God's word. As a result, I came to rely upon scripture alone. The knowledge gained from the Bible now gave me the confidence to use the Bible as the only authority for my faith. I regarded the Bible as my 'emergency flight manual.'

"In pilot training, we were told to 'trust our flight manuals and the procedures that had been established within them,' because those procedures had already been tested over time. We also understood that the flight manual kept us from making the same deadly mistakes that others have made.

"I did not leave my Catholic faith because of what the Bible said; I left my Catholic faith because of the things the Church was teaching that did not line up with the teachings of scripture. I have been teaching a Bible study class for ten years, and over eighty percent of my class is ex-Catholic. I grew up with religion; the Bible now pointed me in the direction of a saving relationship with Jesus Christ. I still pray for those who remain blinded to the simplicity of the gospel and the incredible life that is immediately offered to every man, woman, or child who comes to know Jesus Christ as Savior and Lord."[1]

When I was an infant, God as I knew Him had been delivered to me by the Church's beliefs and practices. Naturally and instinctively, we revert to what is instilled in each of us. Many Catholics and former Catholics as well, battle with that same instinct. God took me on an amazing journey of discovery and has brought me to a wonderful point in my life where He again, dramatically got my attention. Through a strange turn of events I often questioned and protested, it is only now I understand why they took place; to share with you through this book my discovery, a better way to live life.

The opportunity before you now is yours to grab onto and realize a new way of living. I tell you the truth; I am living proof of what God can do in your life if you let Him in. I am no one special or different from anyone else; I have the same wants, needs, and desires as you do. I am an ordinary person; the only difference is that my priorities are now in order. My belief structure is built on a rock-solid foundation of truth, which is God's word. That makes living everyday life so much easier because God is in control, not me.

The truth is, Jesus is waiting for you to accept Him into your circle of close friends. Your relational immaturity with Him will keep you powerless and ineffective in having control over your life; He wants and desires a personal relationship with you. Being a good person, getting religion and doing the right things never brought anyone closer to God or God closer to him or her. Sure, these may help you feel good about yourself for a short time. However, until you act and do something drastic to fill the gap caused by sin, nothing will ever change. I have learned that God hates to be separated from us. In fact, He wants us to enjoy His safety, His peace, and freedom from guilt.

John Strelecky, author of *The Why Café*, published by Da Capo Lifelong Books 2006, makes an interesting comment as he explains his concept called "The Big Five for Life." He says, "People struggle to figure out how to get from where they are at to where they want to go, they face all kinds of obstacles, roadblocks and learning curves. Usually, after the second or third obstacle on the way to their destination, they get discouraged and give up. They are a "Mad How" disease casualty."

Streleckly goes on to explain, "When you know where you are at, and you know where you want to go, the question you need to ask is not how. The question is, who. I can guarantee, with nearly one hundred percent certainty, that some person at some point in the history of the planet has done, seen, or experienced whatever you want to do, see, or experience. All you have to do is find that person, or someone who knows about them, and ask what they did. Then you simply imitate it."[2]

Undeniably, it can be as simple as John says. You have now walked in my shoes so learn from my faults. The average American's life span is 27,740 days.[3] The odometer is clicking away your days right now. I have experienced that how you act, speak and treat others every day is your response to God in action. You have a great opportunity starting right now, to love with authenticity and connect relationally with Jesus as you step across the bridge He built for you. When you do this one simple act, you will find His love not only flowing through you, but also to your spouse, your family, your work, your personal problems, and life in general. This is the secret to living a better life, friends. I tried to make it exceptionally complicated, when realistically, all I needed was an open mind and the will to accept Jesus on a genuine and personal level.

Notably I have come to recognize from Jesus' teachings in the Bible and through the Protestant church that the scriptures are authentic and come directly from God. I hope you are capable of letting go of the pride, the laws of man and our individual reliance and interpretations of what we personally consider is God's word, in order to follow God's word.

Chapter fifteen contains a straightforward illustration of the bridge that God has built for you. He is waiting for you to simply cross over that bridge. Jeremiah 29:13 says, "You will seek me and find me when you seek me with all your heart." It is up to you. We have a short time on this earth, and we have been given the greatest gift of all from God—His son.

Remember, it's all about a relationship. Seize the day. Live a better life by accepting the gift that is offered. Grab the best that life can offer and go for the gusto by letting Jesus into your life.

STUDY GUIDE QUESTIONS

CHAPTER FOURTEEN

Changing Course

GROUP OR CLASS LEADER: Review chapter thirteen. This is the beginning of section six. Ask the group what they have learned up to this point. Ask several people to share something in their life that required courage. Was the outcome a positive or negative one? How did they feel afterwards?

Q: If a storm in your life came up, are you secure in the foundation you have built for yourself? Explain below what you think a solid life foundation looks like in Jesus' eyes.

Q: What happens to people when their belief structure is weak?

Q: When a storm comes crashing down on you, such as a loved one's death, a lost job, stress at work, or a divorce, where do you turn for safety? Do you seek security in the old places where you feel comfortable? Take a moment and think where you turn for comfort. Is it material things, a drink, perhaps something that gives you instant gratification. Explain your thoughts.

Q: Who are you when no one is looking? Are you pleased with who that person is? Why or why not?

Q: You can use your current struggles to grow in faith and find God, or just tread water in anger, searching for something to fill the void that lingers within. What struggles have you had to overcome?

Q: Are you certain the "life preserver" you are clinging to will save you from life's storms? If yes, in what way?

Q: Are you willing to step out of your comfort zone spiritually to accept Christ as your life preserver? In what way?

Q: What have you learned from this chapter?

Q: Are you different from when you started this study guide? What has changed in your life?

Q: Growing and maturing in Christ is a life-long process. Are you willing to make the commitment by stepping up into another stage of growth and renewal in your life? _____

Q: Are you willing to change course and live a better life by accepting Jesus as your Lord and Savior by being re-baptized? _____

Continue to chapter fifteen to begin your adventure with Christ.

The Bridge To Victory
Charting Your Own Course

IN THE BEGINNING, LIFE WAS PERFECT
Man was created for a relationship with God:
No obstacles or barriers
MAN and GOD

BUT NOW, NOT EVERYTHING IS PERFECT AND MAN HAS A PROBLEM

Man has broken the relationship with God because we have chosen to sin against God rather than serve Him. We sin by doing what God has commanded us not to do or by not doing what God has told us to do. We have drifted into thinking that everything is about me.

OUR SIN separates us from God. The penalty for sin is death.

OUR SIN

GOD

DEATH

Man has tried to fill the gap by substituting "things" in order to fill the gap.

Keynote: Church is included in the above list of things used to fill the gap because many people only go through the motions at church. They pretend it helps them feel better and assume they are doing what God wants.

BUT NOTHING CAN FILL THE TRUE NEED.
Then how can we ever have eternal life?

"For it is by grace you have been saved, through faith and this not from yourselves, it is the gift of God: not by works, so that no one can boast." Ephesians 2: 8, 9.

What man could not do, God has done.
God has provided an answer, in his son, Jesus.

"For God so loved the world that he gave his one and only Son, that whoever believes in him shall not perish but have eternal life." John 3:16.

How do you cross the bridge?
You must repent your sins and put your trust in Christ by making him your Lord and Savior.

If you have chosen to walk across the bridge to begin an adventure building a personal relationship with Jesus, or you are not sure how to proceed, simply go to a quiet place where you will not be distracted. While there pause for a moment and seriously contemplate what you are about to do—I suggest you go to a place where no one can find you, and get on your knees. With a contrite and sincere heart, ask God to forgive your sins. Tell Him you are sorry for all of the wrong you have done and confess the hurt you have brought to others and to yourself.

Next, ask Jesus to come into your heart and your life. Simply tell Him He is truly the Lord over and the Savior of your life.

At this point, I suggest you contact your senior pastor or a minister at the church you are attending or thinking about attending, and tell him or her you have accepted Jesus as your Lord and Savior. Explain that you would like to be baptized, as Jesus was, by immersion. If you are not comfortable talking to a church leader, do not hesitate to talk to a Christian friend and explain what you want to do.

IMPORTANT NOTE, there is no reason to be embarrassed; you may be feeling uncomfortable because it is not common for you to be talking about Jesus outwardly. I used to think and feel the same way. Trust me, no one will look at you strangely. Would you be embarrassed to tell Jesus that He is your Lord and Savior if you were to die today? No! So why be embarrassed now? This is not about what others might think. God knows your heart; do not let your actions show differently because you are worried what others may think.

Take this book and diagram with you if it will help explain to your friend, the senior pastor, or minister what you want to accomplish. He or she will welcome you warmly and answer any questions. If you chose to talk to a friend first, it may be a good idea to ask your friend to go with you when you talk to the senior minister.

Lastly, be courageous. Remember, Jesus' goodness drew people to Him. Unfortunately, we have moved the principles back to our own liking by doing our own thing and not His. Catholics and non-Catholics alike, we all have the same Father. We all wrestle with the same problems in life, but we all did not pursue the same objective, which was becoming fully devoted followers of Jesus Christ. Many of us became followers of the church, but when you accept to follow Him, you will witness a life change that will transform you forever. God gave you a mind and soul that are free to choose, but unfortunately, our culture, self-reliance, and pride can interfere with our choice. Why let your ego stand in the way of a better way to live life?

In our current lives, we struggle with personal evils and problems daily. Why continue on a meaningless journey? Come to know the joy of Jesus in your life.

CHAPTER FIFTEEN

The Bridge To Victory

GROUP OR CLASS LEADER: Review chapter fourteen and take time for prayer. Ask God to bless each person who has attended this study. Pray that each individual will open his or her heart to accept Jesus as his or her personal Lord and Savior.

IMPORTANT NOTE:
Encourage those who choose to be baptized to do it as a group.

Assist in explaining the Bridge to Victory. Walk through the process with the whole group (if needed). Ask who would like to set a time to be baptized. Write down each person's name and phone number. Contact your pastor. Next, contact each person on the list personally and give him or her a date and time.

Q: Ask the group what was their biggest take away from this book.

THINK ON THIS: Acts 4:20 "For we cannot help speaking about what we have seen and heard."

If this book was helpful in your journey please share it with your loved ones and friends.

If you are an individual struggling with accepting Christ in your life, contact me at www.GrowingUpCatholic.net

Notes

Disaster Strikes Home

1. Matthew Pg. 1439; Mark Pg. 1490; Luke 1532, NIV.
2. John 3:3 NIV, 1598.

Facing the Facts

1. *"American Religious Identification Survey,"* by The Graduate Center of the City University of New York, Copyright 2006. Exhibit #9 29 of 47. www.gc.cuny.edu/faculty/research_studies/aris.pdf
2. CNN Transcript aired with Aaron Brown and Vatican Analyst John Allen, April 4, 2005. *Thousands Pay Respects to Pope; American Catholics Welcome Change in Practices.*
3. IDEM..
4. *American Religious Identification Survey*, by the Graduate Center of the City University of New York, Copyright 2006. Exhibit #1, pg 25 of 47.http://www. gc.cuny.edu/faculty/research_studies/aris.pdf.
5. CNN Newsroom, Vatican Sexual Abuse Scandal, April 7, 2010. Posted at 8:44 a.m. http://newsroom.blogs.cnn.com/2010/04/07/vatican-sex-abuse-scandal/
6. *Bishop Accountability*. USA Today/AP February 10, 2004. By Cathy Lynn Grossman, Copyright 2004. www.usatoday.com/news/nation/2004-02-10-priestsabuse_x.htm. Used by permission

Purgatory – Temporary Punishment

1. *The Canons and Decrees of the Council of Trent* by Rev. H.J. Schroder, editor Copyright 1978 by Tan Books. Rev. ed. 2005. Twenty-Fifth Session. p 214. ISBN 0-89555-074-1
2. *Bob and Josie German story*. Dr Joseph Mizzi author. Website: www.justforcatholics.org. Used by permission.
3. *Catholic Customs and Traditions*, by Greg Dues, Copyright 2005 Rev. ed. ISBN 0-8962-2432-5 Twenty-Third Publications, New London, CT.
4. *Catechism of the Catholic Church for Adults*. USCCB Publishing Copyright 2006, 161.
5. H.J. Schroeder, trans. ***The Canons and Decrees of the Council of Trent.*** Copyright 1978. Tan Books. 46.
6. Pope Paul VI, *Indulgentiarum Doctrina*, January 1, 1967. www.Catholic-pages.com. Chapter 1, paragraph 4. Provided Courtesy of: Eternal Word Television Network.
7. Matthew 20:28 NIV, 1471
8. 2 Timothy 2:12 NIV, 1845
9. 1 John 1:7 NIV, 1908

Confession – Or Compensation

1. *Canons and Decrees of the Council*, H.J. Schroeder, Trans. Copyright 2006 ISBN 0-89555-074-1 *Canons Concerning the Most Holy Sacrament of Penance*, Canon 7. 103.
2. OP. CIT., 93.
3. Romans 3:20 NIV. 1709

4. *Fast Facts on Roman Catholicism*, by John Ankerberg and John Weldon, 73.
   Copyright 2004. ISBN 978-1-57455-720-6
5. Colossians 2:13 1815 NIV
6. *The Roman Catholic Teaching on Salvation and Justification*, by William Webster.
7. Titus 3:5 NIV 1853
8. What the Bible is all About, by Dr. Henrietta C. Mears.
   Copyright 1997. 707. Copyright © 2nd. ed.
   Gospel Light, Ventura, CA 93003. Used by permission.

Saints as Our Intercessors
1. Catechism of the Catholic Church, op. cit., para 962, 54.
2. Dr Joseph Mizzi, *Therese Salzburg Story*. Used by permission
   web site: www.justforcatholics.org
3. John 14:6 1625 NIV.
4. Catechism of Catholic Church, op.cit., para 957, 249ff.
5. Idem, para 828, 219.
6. Matthew 28:18 1489 NIV.
7. John 5:22 1604 NIV.
8. Ephesians 1:20 1792 NIV.

Queen of Heaven
1. *Catholic Encyclopedia*, transcribed by Robert Gordon. *The
   Catholic Encyclopedia, Volume I* Copyright 1907. Required
   the clergy to ensure that the faithful recited the Hail Mary.
2. Dr. John Ankerberg and Dr. John Weldon, *The Biblical, Catholic, and
   Occult View of Mary*. Dr. Ankerberg is President and founder of The
   Ankerberg Theological Research Institute Producer and host of the
   nationally televised John Ankerberg Show, a half-hour program seen in
   all 50 states via independent stations. www.johnankerberg.org/Articles/
   romancatholicism-/RC0300W4.htm" www.johnankerberg.org/Articles/
   romancatholicism-/RC0300W4.htm. 5th paragraph down.
3. *The Origin of the Rosary*, by Mike McCormack, National Historian.
   The Catholic Forum, Anthony of Padua, Patron saint.
   www.aoh.com/history/archive/rosary.htm
4. *South Florida Sun Sentinel*, Broward metro ed. Foreign Section A10.
   Aug. 9, 2006 by Krzysztof Kopacz. Associated Press.
5. *Into The Light*, Dr. John Lerma, M.D. 2007 by Career Press Inc. N. J.
   ISBN-13: 978-56414-972-5.
6. John 17:5 NIV. 1629.
7. *The New American Catholic Bible*, 1984-85 ed.
   Copyright 1981 Devore & Sons, Inc. Wichita, Kansas 67201. *Life of the
   Blessed Virgin Mary,* 1164.
8. IDEM
9. Apostolic Constitution *Munificenitssimus Deus*.
   Defining the Dogma of the Assumption, POPE PIUS XII. November 1,
   1950. Libreria Editrice Vaticana.

Section three – Obligated to Obey

1. *Church in Search of Itself*, by Robert Blair Kaiser, Copyright 2006. ISBN: 0375410643. Robert Kaiser has been writing about the Catholic Church since 1962, when *Time* magazine sent him to Rome to cover the Second Vatican Ecumenical Council. He was a contributing editor for *Newsweek*.
2. CNN Transcript, OP. CIT.

The Authority of the Council

1. http://en.wikipedia.org/wiki/Council_of_Trent
2. Phillip Schaff, The History of The Christian Church (Hendrickson Publishers, Inc., 1996, originally published 1892), Vol. 8, 600.
3. Way of Life, *Declarations of the Council of Trent*. www.wayoflife.org/fbns/trent.htm. First para.
4. *New American Bible*, Copyright 1981.
5. *Catholic Undertow* by Mary Ann Collins, Copyright 2004. ISBN-13: 978-0595320059, www.catholicundertow.com. Used by permission.
6. Schroeder, transcript. OP. CIT.,18
7. *The ForeRunner*, by Jay Rogers. forerunner.com/chalcedon/X0020_15._Council_of_Trent.html. 2nd paragraph. *The ForeRunner* is a nationally distributed university campus newspaper published by Maranatha Ministries in Gainesville, Florida. Mr. Rogers attended UMASS/Amherst, and double majored in English and Psychology.

Catholic Doctrine vs. the Bible

1. The Gideons International. The primary function of *The Gideons* is placing and distributing Bibles and New Testaments in human traffic lanes and streams of national life.
2. *Catholic Doctrine vs. the Bible* was compiled by Richard Bennett, a converted Catholic priest and now an evangelist. Used with permission. P.O. Box 192 Del Valle, TX 78617. His website is www.bereanbeacon.org.

A Meal to Remember

1. *Dictionary of the Liturgy*, Rev. Jovian P. Lang, OFM., 1989 by Catholic Book Publishing Co., N. Y. ISBN 0-8994-2273-X
2. *The Ten Most Common Liturgical Abuses and Why They're Wrong*, Kevin Orlin Johnson. Taken from the featured article in *This Rock* magazine from Catholic Answers. www.catholic.com/thisrock/1999/9901fea1.asp.

I Have a Decision to Make

1. Corinthians 15:1-2, p.1755
2. Matthew 3:17, p.1446
3. *Baptism: Immersion Only?* Baptism in the Early Church. www.catholic.com/library/Baptism_Immersion_Only.asp
4. *How to become a Christian*, question #14. www.johnankerberg.com. By John Ankerburg.
5. Tim and Angie Hollinden, personal story of Baptism. Used by permission, August 2006.
6. Personal story by Debbie Tuggle. Used by permission, September 2006.

What Do I Say to My Family?
1. Personal story by Debbie DeMont. Used by permission, October 2006.
2. Personal story by Micki Jerry. Used by permission, July 2006.

An Alternative Choice
1. *God: The Evidence* by Patrick Glynn Copyright 2006. ISBN 0-7615-0941-0. Patrick is a former atheist with a Ph.D. from Harvard and is the associate director and scholar in residence at the George Washington University Institute for Communitarian Policy Studies, in Washington, D.C.

Changing Course – Taking the Next Step
1. Personal Story, "*Saved at 33,000 Feet*," by Rick Michelena. Used by permission, November 2006. Copyright 2000-2006 Dr. Joseph Mizzi.
2. John Strelecky, author of *The Why Café*. International Best-selling author of "*The Why Café*." ISBN-13: 978-0-738-1063-6. Copyright 2003. www.whycafe.com. John is a highly sought after inspirational speaker on "How to Achieve Maximum Success with Minimal Effort."
3. Source: *Social Security Statistical Tables*. Updated April 6, 2006. www.ssa.gov/ OACT/STATS/index.html.

Quick Order Form

Email orders: www.GrowingUpCatholic.net

Postal orders: Abundant Publishing Company
PO Box 770816
Coral Springs, FL 33077, USA

Telephone: 954-822-4995.

Fax orders: 866-376-7137. Send this form.

Name:_____

Address:_____

City:_____ State:_____ Zip:_____

Telephone:_____

Email address:_____

Sales tax: Please add 6% if you live in Florida.

Standard shipping: (7 to 10 days) $2.00 per book, 75 cents for each additional book.

Priority shipping: (2 to 3 days) $4.05 per book. For additional books contact for shipping costs.

International: Contact for shipping cost.

ATTENTION CHURCHES: Quantity discounts are available on bulk purchases of this book for educational, gift purposes, or for small groups.

ABOUT THE AUTHOR

Tim Lott and his wife Genora make their home in South Florida. He grew up as a Catholic in Louisville, Kentucky.

Tim worked in various fields and locations from St. Simons, Georgia, to starting a business with his father and brother, Lott System, Inc., in Louisville.

Tim accepted Christ as Savior in October 1998 and was baptised on December 21, 1998. Tim worked on staff at Northeast Christian Church in Louisville, Kentucky, as Director of Ministries and in 2003, he became an ordained minister. After transferring to Florida in 2005 he worked as the Minister of Involvement at Community Christian Church of Fort Lauderdale, Florida.

Tim Lott

Tim started teaching the "Growing Up Catholic" class in 2002 at Northeast. He has a passion for connecting people into the local church, assisting Catholics and former Catholics alike in discovering a better way to live life instead of merely going through the motions on Sunday mornings.

Tim is now a hospice chaplain working for Vitas Innovative Hospice Care in South Florida. In his spare time, he enjoys road biking and sailing with his wife along with spending time at the beach.